— Praise for —
The Art of Pacing

"Every runner knows the danger of going out too fast. Managing your pace is the key to fulfilling your potential. *The Art of Pacing* shows us how that same principle governs work, relationships, and life itself. This book is a much-needed antidote to hustle culture, which has left many of us burned out or disengaged. Svoboda expertly draws on science, sports, and real-world stories to argue that the path to a meaningful life isn't about going harder. It's about going wiser."

—Steve Magness, author of *Do Hard Things* and *Win the Inside Game*

"*The Art of Pacing* is a wise and welcome antidote to hustle culture. Blending science, research, and storytelling, Svoboda makes a compelling case that the secret to thriving in the modern world is not to speed everything up or slow it all down. It's to find the right pace—for the task, the moment, the life you wish to lead. Because mastering the art of pacing is how you master the art of living."

—Carl Honoré, author of *In Praise of Slowness*

"Engaging and deeply reported, *The Art of Pacing* is essential reading for anyone who seeks to work hard without burning out."

—Olga Khazan, author of *Me, But Better*

"At a moment when speed is often mistaken for progress, Svoboda shows that pacing isn't a luxury—it's a prerequisite for doing meaningful work in the long run. This book is a salve for a world that has forgotten how to slow down."

—Simone Stolzoff, author of *The Good Enough Job* and *How to Not Know*

"*The Art of Pacing* names the lie at the heart of modern ambition: that your only choices are burnout or disengagement. Svoboda offers a smarter, saner, science-backed alternative to grind culture—a way to move through life with intention, energy, and staying power by finding your right pace. Grounded in interdisciplinary research, this practical, approachable guide to flourishing is essential reading for anyone who wants to contribute meaningfully yet sustainably, without sacrificing themselves in the process."

—Megan Hellerer, author of *Directional Living*

The Art of Pacing

A Guide to Balancing
Short-Term Demands
with Long-Term Thriving

Elizabeth Svoboda

Simon Acumen

New York   Amsterdam/Antwerp   London
Toronto   Sydney/Melbourne   New Delhi

SIMON
ACUMEN

An Imprint of Simon & Schuster, LLC
1230 Avenue of the Americas
New York, NY 10020

First Simon Acumen hardcover edition June 2026

SIMON ACUMEN and colophon are registered trademarks of Simon & Schuster, LLC

For information about special discounts for bulk purchases, please contact Simon & Schuster Special Sales at 1-866-506-1949 or business@simonandschuster.com.

The Simon & Schuster Speakers Bureau can bring authors to your live event. For more information or to book an event, contact the Simon & Schuster Speakers Bureau at 1-866-248-3049 or visit our website at www.simonspeakers.com.

Interior design by Laura Levatino

Manufactured in the United States of America

10 9 8 7 6 5 4 3 2 1

Library of Congress Control Number: 2026000718

ISBN 978-1-6680-2241-2
ISBN 978-1-6680-2243-6 (ebook)

Scan here to get book recommendations, exclusive offers, and more delivered to your inbox.

To my children,
who set their own pace and inspire me to follow suit.

Contents

The Art of Pacing

Introduction

As the early sun glints through a scrim of trees, entrants in the Boston Trail Half Marathon swing into their pre-race routines. Some stretch their hamstrings, with legs up on fences beside the trail, which snakes along Pennsylvania's Youghiogheny River. Others pin their printed race numbers onto their jerseys. Amid the commotion, Jim Crist mounts a "MARATHON PACING" banner to an ancient Pittsburgh & Lake Erie railcar, zip-tying it against the rising wind. For more than a decade, veteran marathoner Crist and his handpicked pacing team have helped runners titrate their speed and energy levels throughout long-distance races, allowing them to log strong times with their bodies and minds intact. They focus more on helping runners meet their personal goals than on propelling them past everyone else.

Fifteen minutes before the starting gun, Crist's phalanx of pacers emerges from the crowd, assembling in a row behind the starting line. Each pacer holds up a poster board with a projected finish time printed in black letters. The swiftest runners will stick with veteran marathon pacer Elijah Shekinah, aiming to finish in one hour and forty minutes or less. Those looking to hit the two-hour mark will run with pacer Mike Salamon, and more leisurely entrants will target a two-and-a-half-hour finish with pacer Sha Zhao. The pacers' pockets bulge with rubber-banded bundles of energy bars—sustenance for their groups in the race's final stretches.

A race pacer's most important job is to rescue runners from their own worst impulses. Left to their own devices, many racers go out of the blocks hot, flop two-thirds of the way in, and limp to the finish—or even drop out. "Decisions early on that seem small can have a big impact later," Shekinah says. "You decide, 'Maybe I'll go out a little fast, bank some time.' And you learn in the long run that strategy almost never works."

As 9:00 a.m. inches closer, clusters of runners form around each pacer. Some of the race entrants have worked with pacers before; others are opting in on a lark. "If you go out too fast, this is going to turn into the Boston Massacre," Salamon warns his pacing group, promising a Boston tea party if they can keep their adrenaline corked.

The starting blast sounds, and the runners ease into a jog, disappearing around the trail's first bend. By midmorning—after a gauntlet of uphills and downhills, wind blasts and mud puddles—most will loop back around to the trail's head. Their best-laid race plans will have been tested, altered to match trail conditions and their bodies' fluid demands.

For distance runners, the art of pacing is as essential as breathing. While some racers attempt to stay at top speed indefinitely, long courses have a way of flinging these upstarts back to earth: an ice pick headache, a stubborn cramp, an ankle-twisting uphill curve. In a full marathon, "for the first ten miles, you're going to feel great; you're going to want to run faster," Crist says. "But it's a twenty-six-mile event, and in this business we have a saying: 'If you leave me before mile ten, I guarantee I will pass you before mile twenty.'"

Race collapses that stem from pacing errors are often sudden and definitive. If you start too fast and try to maintain that pace despite your body's protests, your legs will turn so leaden they will barely function. It's easy to see how a too-vigorous start portends a crash two-thirds of the way in, or—on a longer timescale—how fuel and rest the week before a race predict finish times on race day. Those foreseeable outcomes motivate runners to exercise control over their speed during a race, as well as map out training rhythms in the days and weeks beforehand.

For outsiders looking in, what's striking is how effortlessly trained runners navigate the entire pacing spectrum, from stillness to all-out sprints. They are exquisitely attuned to the difference between a 50 and a 75 percent effort, to the level of physical drag a ten-degree slope will impose. They subtly adjust their speed to match course conditions and their energy reserves, much as radio operators home in on the precise frequency they seek. And they maintain a keen sense of how much ground they have still to cover.

Yet outside the sporting realm, the art of regulating your tempo is less intuitive, and the connection between early moves and late-breaking returns is less clear. It's hard to gauge or predict how a marathon night to meet a work deadline will affect your ability to focus or contribute the following week—or how working seventy-hour weeks will affect your stamina, motivation, or well-being years down the line.

As a result, most of us lack the runner's well-tuned sense of when to go hard, when to pull back, and when to stay the course. We jump into big, critical projects and end up mentally fried a week or two in, sabotaged by a too-keen zeal to make overnight progress. We get in a work-from-home lull of scrolling social media feeds, fall far behind, then compensate with a last-minute sprint, heading far past the limits of exhaustion. Or we hew stubbornly to familiar tempos and marked paths, shunning detours that would renew and strengthen us.

More fundamentally, we often try to sustain a punishing pace for many years, muffling any distress signals that crop up along the way. This affliction is widespread in cultures that value the speed and cachet of any given pursuit more than its substance or meaning, and those that lionize superhuman effort while downplaying questions of who all that effort serves or how it changes the larger picture.

What's more, we don't always connect our pacing errors to their ultimate consequences. We suffer through chronic health issues—anxiety, sleeplessness, high blood pressure—yet fail to see how they are linked to going too hard, with too nebulous a sense of what all the grinding is for. Or we feel guilty and aimless after months of disengaged drifting, but we lack a clear sense of what to do next. As a result, we tend to make the same pacing mistakes over and over, wary of ceding ground to correct course.

Whether on the course or off, deliberate pacing begins with an unsparing willingness to connect your daily decisions to their potential longer-term outcomes. When aspiring runners call Jim Crist to ask if he and his team can help them with pacing, Crist conducts what amounts to a full case history over phone or video chat. He records each data point in painstaking detail: how many races they've run before, their past times, how much they've been training (and resting) during the past few months.

New runners often approach Crist with lofty goals: a top ten finish, a spot in a premier event like the Boston Marathon. In response, he asks them to explain what kind of preparation they've done so far. "At times I'll say, 'That sounds solid,'" Crist says. "Other times, 'I think you're not realistic about where you are physically.'" Sustainable pacing, in short, requires a frank initial analysis of where you are now, what your desired goal is, and whether you have the resources and stamina to make it there.

Next, Crist guides his runners in setting a flexible schedule of exertion and rest in the weeks leading up to the race. The amount of downtime he advises seems surprising to some of them, but Crist stresses—with a confidence born of hard-won experience—that neglecting rest is akin to self-sabotage. "You have to have a master plan. I know myself that I should take two or three days off a week," he says. Head-down stretches of training, however, are equally as crucial. This focused effort enables athletes to run better than they ever expected they could—the kind of exhilarating feat that drew many of them to the sport in the first place, and one that has little to do with besting other runners.

But outside the athletic realm, conversations about pacing often lack this kind of nuance and balance, gravitating instead toward extremes. One set of influencers celebrates grind culture and going 110 percent, urging people to push past feelings of exhaustion because the end result will make the pain worthwhile. Other voices, just as loud, urge people to "quiet quit," "lie flat," or otherwise disengage.

These messages may be helpful, even necessary, in the right context. But research also highlights the benefits of operating in multiple pace registers rather than solely at the binary extremes. The 110 percent road is littered with the bodies and minds of many who remained on that course at all costs. And while the prospect of dropping out or "quiet quitting" may be seductive, calls for total stillness clash with studies showing that some degree of challenge—engaging in pursuits that are big and meaningful—is essential to happiness and fulfillment. What's more, as runners have long known, certain kinds of active engagement are restorative in ways stillness can never be, and certain kinds of retreat are more stressful than relaxing.

Finding the proper pace for each moment, what Slow Movement pioneer Carl Honoré calls the *tempo giusto*, involves a delicate dance between engagement and withdrawal, between self-transcendence and self-protection.

The ideal Aristotle called *eudaimonia*, which involves making meaningful contributions that serve some greater good, resides in the neglected middle of the pacing spectrum, the territory just a few people traverse while millions gravitate toward absolutes. While traversing this middle range—the vast stretch between going beyond and dropping out—takes self-scrutiny and the courage to buck cultural norms, it is also a healthy default zone that fuels long-term thriving. Those who master the middle of the spectrum are productive and engaged, but they reject the notion of productivity as an idol or an end in itself. Instead, they view it as a means of building a life with an impact that outlasts its duration.

In recent years, interest in this less-traversed stretch of the spectrum has soared. As people transitioned to work-from-home schedules in the wake of the COVID pandemic, they found themselves thriving at a less hurried pace that they never would have chosen outright. It's in such moments of inflection—glimpses of a different life, set in contrast to old, frantic rhythms—that chances for meaningful negotiation can arise.

As unfamiliar as it might feel, measured pace-setting sounds good to most of us, at least in theory. It's the implementation that tends to trip us up. "We don't learn how to pace ourselves," says organizational change consultant Emily Masters Rosenthal. "There's not a class on that."

To be sure, time-management approaches abound, from the Pomodoro method of churning out twenty-five-minute work blocks to scheduling prompts that map your day in fifteen-minute increments. While slicing days into precise snippets can help mark progress, this approach backfires when it becomes too unbending, since unexpected events large and small can, within minutes, upend weeks of orderly planning.

Many popular time-management methods lull us into believing we're pacing ourselves when what we're actually doing is boxing ourselves in. Meticulous schedule charting trains us to zero in on the minutiae of planning our days, rather than on the larger business of where we're headed. More resilient pacing approaches reject this scheduling rigidity. They can accommodate evolving decisions about how to spend each day, hour, or minute. They involve recognizing when familiar, entrenched rhythms aren't working or when inner reserves are running low, and then shifting course accordingly.

In the final days before any big event, pacer Mike Salamon says, it's crucial to acknowledge your limits and take training breaks when you feel you can't go another step. "This isn't the time to improve your fitness. It's time to hold back and keep your sanity." If you exhaust your body and mind too much during practice, he explains, you'll have few reserves left to draw on when you tackle the last miles of a long race.

Like Crist's and Salamon's approach to marathon training, the pacing tactics this book outlines are preemptive. They involve acknowledging physical and mental limits from the outset, rather than disregarding them until they can't be denied. They proceed in time with natural biological rhythms, rather than suppressing them. They take cues from cultures that embrace the kind of deep retreat that spurs transformative action. And they are flexible enough to accommodate whatever daily obstacles might arise.

In a nod to pacing's athletic roots, this book is loosely structured like a long-distance race. The first section is a research-based analysis of our default pacing habits and the physical and existential tolls they exact. This section ends with strategies that help you define what kind of course you want to pursue, since pacing becomes easier and more natural when you have a clearer idea about where you're headed.

The following chapters explore how to pace yourself once you've embarked on your chosen course. You'll learn about pacing strategies that are appropriate for a range of pursuits, from work to community service to online engagement, and you'll hear from business leaders, Olympic athletes, and ordinary people who use these tactics regularly. Some of these strategies are geared toward alternating periods of rest and focused effort, while others show you how to direct your focused efforts in ways that energize you rather than deplete you. As I investigate the gamut of pacing strategies, I test some of them for myself and report on how well they work in real life.

The final chapters address how to sustain a lifelong commitment to smart pacing, which often means reassessing your speed or approach as your goals and objectives evolve.

This book resists defining pacing as a standard self-improvement venture. Instead of showing you how to extract maximum efficiency from your body and mind, it encourages you to pace yourself toward reaching the rich, meaning-filled life Aristotle envisioned, rather than juicing your productivity or grabbing the status ring.

Researchers say that people who live like this are "flourishing." Flourishing implies much more than happiness or pleasure. It also involves serving the community in ways that energize you and that suit your unique strengths—making a contribution that endures. It's locating your place in a larger, interconnected whole and nurturing the relationships that allow you to maintain that place.

Rooted in contribution rather than primacy, flourishing subverts the breakneck-pace credo insisting that what counts is perpetually coming out ahead. In the face of national and global crises, from habitat destruction to creeping autocracy, those who pace themselves toward flourishing are best prepared to generate shared solutions and commit to those solutions for the long haul. In this way, astute individual pacing can give rise to astute collective pacing.

Though pacer Elijah Shekinah crosses the line at around the one-hour-forty-minute mark—the precise time he was aiming for—his group's finishing push didn't materialize quite the way he'd planned. At the beginning of the race, "usually you want to go steady," he says. "It didn't go like that. We kept beating our estimates." Since his group had a strong wind at their backs for the first half of the race, they went out faster than they typically would have, and he had to remind them to pull back. But when the trail looped around and the wind was whipping into their eyes, things got tougher, and the energy they had banked earlier had to propel them to the finish.

More than twenty minutes later, pacer Mike Salamon limps across the line, sucking wind. He had pledged to come in at two hours on the dot, but that didn't happen because he had trouble taking a full, deep breath in the late stretches of the race. His chest clenched just when he wanted to surge forward, and he had to ratchet down his speed to make it to the finish. "Three years ago," he says, "I was a one-hour-fifty-minute pacer on a hotter day, and I did fine."

Visceral limits like Salamon's may be confounding and unpredictable, but they are as obdurate as walls when they do arise. By resisting the impulse to blaze past such limits, shrewd pacers in all domains can resist the kinds of all-out crashes—physical or existential—that take weeks or months to overcome.

Psychologist Rollo May defines freedom as the ability to slow down or pause long enough to choose the ideal course of action, to respond to what's happening in ways that both preserve the self and expand its boundaries. The pace adjustments that are second nature to distance runners offer this kind of freedom, giving you room to pursue meaningful goals while evading the breakdowns that so often seem like the price of admission. As May intuited, pacing is a moral endeavor as well as a practical one: It sustains you, equipping you to sustain and nourish what matters most.

As the final pacing group—the two-and-a-half-hour group—crosses the finish line to the sound of cowbells, their leader, pacer Sha Zhao, is practically skipping. "How did you do?" she shouts to Salamon.

"Not so good!"

"You showed up!" Zhao returns, grinning impishly.

"Best pacer ever!" a runner named Keith shouts, jogging up to Zhao and clapping her on the back. Zhao saved him from his most overzealous self at the right moments, Keith says, keeping him from setting a pace he couldn't maintain. And she stressed practical necessities he was tempted to overlook in his race-day trance. "She's like, 'You're going to stop at the water station!' She brought us back to reality."

The art of pacing involves venturing back to reality—continually and in myriad ways. It's essentially a Stoic art, a commitment to seeing things as they are and changing course when socially sanctioned tempos no longer suffice. Pacing allows you to pursue meaningful goals at your own rate and on your own terms, steering clear of hand-me-down ideas about where you should be headed and when you should get there. Pacing rebukes cultural worship of the grind and instead embraces recovery practices that fuel thoughtful, necessary action, which can make it akin to principled dissent. Fluency in the full range of the pacing spectrum means mastering expansion and contraction alike. Everything is subject to movement and negotiation, and it's that negotiation that allows for life-long flourishing.

Chapter 1

A Breakneck Pace

When I was in kindergarten, my Montessori teacher—who was tall, bespectacled, and perpetually in command—showed me how to solve a math problem. He sat down with me at a low table, wrote out the steps on a piece of paper, then added another, similar problem for me to try. Following his instructions, I solved it. As I sensed his surprise and absorbed his praise, I felt powerful. It was the same whoosh of excitement I got at our neighborhood barbershop, where you put a lock of hair into a tiny cabinet and opened another door to reveal a plastic prize.

But the older I got, the more I realized that effortless hair-lock exchange had been a myth. To claim the prize that meant most—undivided adult attention, proof I was worth giving a damn about—I had to carry out a precise set of instructions, spoken or unspoken. Blitz through the math test and notch the highest score. Memorize the longest, most detailed poem and recite it. The surest way to open new prize doors was to claim any superlatives on offer—the quickest, the most flawless, the most creative. And that demanded focused labor: sitting at my desk for an hour to perfect a single essay paragraph; reciting my oral book report over and over, forsaking all else, until each spoken word flowed seamlessly into the next.

By middle school, I'd become obsessed with watching gymnastics. Everything about the sport felt oddly familiar: the flawless execution, the routines planned down to the last foot shuffle, the thirty-plus-hour practice weeks. Though I'd never even lowered myself into a split, I identified profoundly with the tiny athletes on parade. As I sat in front of the TV, watching my Barcelona Olympics recording for the hundredth time, my father had a sudden flash of insight: "Do you feel like a scholastic gymnast?"

In the airtight realm of the scholastic gymnast—part self-created, part reinforced by outside voices and metrics—the work I was actually doing felt secondary. The test-taking wasn't the point, nor was the drawing, the writing, or the poetry memorizing. The important thing, perhaps the only thing, that mattered was the reaction I could elicit. The reaction proving that I had won, that I was worthy. Already, my resolve was white-hot: Nothing would prevent me from opening that prize door.

In early life, many of us sprint the first few miles of a marathon without realizing that's what we're doing. No one warns us that this breakneck speed cannot be sustained or that even white-hot resolve depletes. The only pace we learn is the one the system pounds into us as synonymous with success. As midlife creeps up, our fatigue mounts, along with questions about why we're grinding so hard in the first place. But we have little idea how to pause or retreat before the next push, schooled as we are in the gospel of never letting up.

This gospel has an unmistakable subtext: You have to hustle to secure your share because the available goods are limited. When someone else wins a prize, a promotion, or a coveted fellowship, you lose. This zero-sum mindset is so prevalent that even questioning it feels fraught. Yet the unbending ambition it instills—to remain perpetually ahead of the pack—saps the sense of purpose that fuels long-term flourishing. By forsaking culturally sanctioned one-upmanship, you can begin to set a sustainable pace, one tailored to what you actually want to pursue and why.

A Grueling Pace

Being American has always been about going to great lengths to set yourself apart from the rest. For law student Sarah Fisher, growing up in a culture of one-upmanship felt like riding an ever-looping conveyor belt. At her public high school in Nashville, Tennessee, course loads of multiple AP (Advanced Placement) classes were expected, and forgoing sleep to do homework was almost a rite of passage. Throughout her high school years, Fisher felt like she rarely had time to take a break, let alone reflect on where she was headed and what she wanted out of life. "I'd get home and just work on homework," she says, "go to bed, wake up six-ish, and do it all again."

College turned out to be just as grueling. Though Fisher was involved in a mock trial program and the student newspaper, she still had the creeping sense she hadn't mastered the game, that there were other levels she needed to unlock. "Just two clubs didn't look good enough on my résumé. You talk to people who are triple-majoring, and they have all these internships," Fisher says. "It's just feeling like you have to keep pace with every single other person."

The breakneck expectations Fisher faces are inherited, with roots that date back centuries. While crisscrossing the new United States in the 1800s, French philosopher Alexis de Tocqueville noted its citizens' zealous desire for self-perfection, fueled by an unflagging work ethic. He also saw how that desire gave them tunnel vision. In America, "the excitement of competition, the charm of anticipated success, are so many spurs to urge men onward," de Tocqueville wrote, "without allowing them to deviate for an instant from the track."

That tunnel vision propelled many Americans forward. Barely a century after it was founded, America became a world leader in a dizzying array of industries, from manufacturing and refining to shipping and power generation. While laborers, wayfarers, and industrial tycoons occupied different rungs on the status ladder, the common denominator was self-determination taken to its zenith—"to meet life as a powerful conqueror," as poet Walt Whitman wrote, "and nothing exterior shall ever take command of me."

This ideal of self-determination was passed from one generation to the next, thriving in social hubs like schools, churches, and clubs. But while this ideal seemed liberating, it was also constraining, built as it was on the assumption that self-perfection was a life sentence—something you needed to strive perpetually toward. It was un-American to rest on your laurels, to step back and savor what you'd accomplished. Your stature could always be fuller, an axiom that locked people into doing whatever was needed to amplify it.

After automation and offshoring conspired to eliminate millions of jobs in the late twentieth century, a scarcity mindset began to merge with established American ideas about primacy. Surviving in a dog-eat-dog economy, the revised dogma went, meant outcompeting all the others trying to do the same. The goal was to hit all the approved checkpoints as spectators looked on: attending an elite college, graduating with honors, joining a high-end firm, moving to the corner suite. Winning these predefined contests guaranteed a steady stream of praise, while losing, or even faltering, meant you were lazy or just not trying hard enough.

Against this backdrop, writes cultural critic William Deresiewicz, "the purpose of life becomes the accumulation of gold stars," handed out for meeting accepted benchmarks of success. These gold stars are on offer in a vast array of disciplines, not just scholarly ones. Nine- and ten-year-old kids put in double-digit hours a week on travel athletic teams, some sustaining overuse injuries before high school. Other families spend tens of thousands of dollars (or hours) prepping their kids for beauty pageants, rodeos, or debate competitions.

"The five kids in our family were never pushed to be doctors or lawyers or other specific professions, but rather to be the best at what we are," says Mary Westheimer, an author and marketing manager in Phoenix, Arizona. Decades on, though she now sees the wisdom of pulling back, that will to win continues to define her. "'Driven' is my middle name."

The name of the game isn't braininess or athleticism per se. It's asserting some sort of dominance and maintaining that dominance. Grinding is no longer just a means to a larger end; it's also a cardinal virtue in itself, and exhaustion is a sign you're on the right track. Speed and efficiency have become gauges of human value. It's no accident that you have to answer questions at a rapid clip to score well on tests like the SAT.

With the dominance imperative locked in, pursuits that once inspired you often devolve into grim duties—obligations you muscle through, jaw set, until the next fleeting escape. After crashing on a key jump at the World Figure Skating Championships, past US champion Gracie Gold realized she'd kept skating in large part because she felt such pressure from her family and the public to stay on top. Her grueling, elite training regimen, she explained at the time, involved pushing "past the border of normal and into the realm of insanity."

That unrelenting gold-star mindset takes a toll across demographics and social classes. Once they reach their teen years, three in ten kids have perfectionism severe enough to affect their schoolwork and well-being; and in a 2023 Gallup poll of more than 2,400 college students, over half reported feeling worried "during a lot of the day." The stress of achievement culture also disproportionately affects students of color, leading them to consider dropping out of college at higher rates than their peers. It's never been clearer that perpetual one-upmanship contains the seeds of its own destruction.

Born into a striving family in the 1980s, I was a product of this system through and through. I had no inkling how unusual this particular set of values was in human history, and I couldn't imagine what life looked like outside it. I was good at navigating the pre-set checkpoints, which enticed me to buy into the system. I lived to see my name in boldface type in the school newsletter for acing tests or winning science medals. Each time I did, the praise I got locked the cycle of seeking into place.

I can't remember a time when anyone mentioned I ought to step back, recharge, or consider how to direct my energy. Winning all the time wasn't something to celebrate, not really. It was the expected baseline—my own and my community's—and anything less was a deviation. "Every morning in Africa a gazelle wakes up. It knows that it must run faster than the fastest lion or it will be killed," read a yearbook message to a schoolmate of mine from her family. "When the sun comes up, you had better be running!"

From time to time, some vague awareness that none of this was sustainable might surface, like a white whale dimly visible through the depths. This thought seemed heretical, an excuse for sloth, and I racked up a double-digit AP course load to suppress it.

But warning signs were cropping up even before graduation. When I won an overall school art award in my senior year, I had a D average in one art class because I'd stopped doing any assignments at all. Some internal voice, one I couldn't yet acknowledge, was already saying *Enough*.

In college, I signed up for a Great Books program that featured the Western canon's heavy hitters: Plato, Aristotle, Kant, Tolstoy. I would spend the year reflecting on what it meant to live a good life. In principle, I loved that idea. In practice, the program's pace—*War and Peace* in about two weeks—so overwhelmed me that I'd crash on a chair in our dorm suite's common room, willing myself to get through yet another chapter before bed. But the next morning, I'd realize none of it had sunk in. I might as well have been reading the telephone book.

By sophomore year, I felt as if a band had tightened around my solar plexus. I was striving the way I always had, but I wasn't making the same headway. I'd never seen a psychiatrist before, but feeling out of options,

I booked an appointment anyway. My assigned doctor-in-training nodded along, bored, as I talked about my free-floating anxiety. In lieu of practical advice, he wrote me a prescription for Klonopin (clonazepam). I popped a pill and soon wished I hadn't; my eyelids began to droop and my thoughts felt sludgy and recalcitrant. Here I was, in despair because I couldn't keep pace, and this drug had me dozing off by midafternoon. I stuffed the pill bottle deep into a cardboard box, canceled my next appointment, and returned to the business of chasing the next win.

You Had Better Be Running (But Why?)

Once behavioral patterns are laid down, they tend to continue unless something actively interrupts them. In my twenties and thirties, I learned that when I worked through the afternoon and evening, going all out before deadlines, ignoring my needs for food and breaks, I got rewarded with praise and more assignments. And I couldn't shake the sense that if I decided to take the afternoon off—for a long walk or just some reading—someone else, many someones, in fact, were going to eclipse me. "When the sun comes up, you had better be running." Many of my friends whipped themselves the same way. We'd trade war stories about how we'd killed ourselves to make deadlines, and their no-holds-barred pace helped dictate my own.

That kind of social reinforcement makes it easy to sidestep asking yourself exactly what you're aiming for. When you believe that driving hard proves your worth to you and to others, that apparent proof can seem like enough of a reward on its own, at least temporarily. But once that mindset has seized you, it's hard to fathom letting yourself coast or decelerate. You veer ever closer to the prototype of the diligent striver with an underdeveloped sense of purpose—great at getting things done, as Deresiewicz puts it, but less and less sure why you're doing them in the first place.

Over time, that stunted sense of purpose compounds existing pacing problems. When strivers feel unmotivated, they may seesaw between procrastinating and frantically compensating for it, a habit that depletes their reserves still further. "It just turns into a cycle," Sarah Fisher says—one that, for her, became entrenched when sequences of deadlines loomed. "I would get so tired from having to work on one thing that I just didn't want to work the next day. Then I'd put something else off, and I'd have to do another big bout of work to finish that."

That boom-and-bust cycle intensified for me in my thirties. I found myself spacing out on the couch until midmorning, unable to motivate myself to head to my desk. At that point, ashamed of slacking, I'd shut down social media, rush to my computer, and try to tackle my to-do list in half the time I'd planned.

Once in a while, I'd take days off, understanding on some level that I needed to recover from this extreme yo-yoing. But resting often felt unnatural; taking an afternoon off for bookstore browsing went against a lifetime of ingrained programming. The editor and poet Devrupa Rakshit struggles to relax in much the same way, and she marvels at people who can. "Aren't they constantly reminded of every task on their to-do list for the following day, while being simultaneously haunted by every chore they didn't get to?" Yet when I shrank from relaxation and retreat, I couldn't summon the energy I needed to plunge full tilt into my work. As the COVID pandemic crested, I spent longer and longer intervals staring into the middle distance, bobbing in apathetic limbo.

When the term "languishing"—a free-floating state of stagnation—started trending on social media, it felt all too on the nose. Languishing, a term sociologist Corey Keyes coined, "feels as if you're muddling through your days," writes author Adam Grant, "looking at your life through a foggy windshield." Though it doesn't signal an immediate mental-health crisis, it's still a state of malaise; the Latin root of the word, *languere*, denotes "illness."

•   •   •

As I talk to psychologist Christina Maslach about how unchecked striving feeds into our shared malaise, she nods. She's seen it countless times before. "The notion is that if you just cope, that's the solution," says Maslach, author of *The Burnout Challenge*. "You're going to have to figure out how to deal with the heat, you're going to have to be tougher, you're going to have to be more resilient."

But that mindset is precisely the one Maslach has seen drive thousands of people to the edge in their thirties and forties (or even in their twenties). Having learned to lap the track faster than anyone else, they stubbornly try to maintain their early pace—and end up depleted well before middle age, often unsure precisely where they're headed and why. They hit burnout, a profound state of physical and mental exhaustion.

High levels of early-life stress, research shows, can court later burnout, and people who lack a strong "sense of coherence"—a belief that their lives have meaning—are also more likely to crash and burn years down the line. "When the sun comes up, you had better be running" can invert without warning, like an umbrella flipping inside out.

In America, the quintessential society that never sleeps, those who sound the alarm about a win-at-all costs culture tend to get written off as special snowflakes. Feeling wrung out, the nose-to-the-grindstone types insist, is just the price you pay for meeting whatever goal you're striving toward.

But there's a major caveat to this theory that goes ignored. More invested hours yield more returns only up to a certain point. Beyond that point, further efforts don't just fail to move you forward but inch you closer to the kind of collapse that can take months or years to overcome. Stanford researchers report that employees who work seventy hours a week get little more done than those who work forty or fifty hours. People who work more than sixty hours a week, meanwhile, are more likely to get injured at work than their more moderate counterparts, and those who work more than forty-eight hours a week are more likely to become depressed. Overwork, from this standpoint, is about as inefficient as it gets—and understanding this viscerally is key to puncturing our collective discomfort with stillness.

Unchecked striving becomes especially perilous when it's done in the name of self-elevation. People whose chief goal is winning often feel depleted, not just because they have little sense of what their lives stand for beyond triumph but also because they're perpetually unsure of their worth. Though victories might exhilarate them briefly, anything less prompts demoralizing spirals of self-doubt. "The language of winning and losing exhausts us," writes sociologist Francisco Duina, author of *Winning: Notes on an American Obsession.* "Rather than being in harmony with the world, we are drained by it."

Those bent solely on chasing wins tend to feel restless and burned out even when they achieve the results they want. (Consider the long line of Olympic gold medalists who descend into depression soon after their crowning victories.)

A Sustaining Pace

People who pace themselves deliberately open up more room to shape the larger goals they want their striving to serve. What looks like sloth on the surface, research shows, is often the precursor to meaningful engagement and flourishing—not just because rest refuels us, but also because it creates space to consider where to direct our efforts. Jenny Odell, the author of *How to Do Nothing,* calls for setting aside unscheduled time to allow the kind of reflection that fuels engaged activism and contribution. Without regular stretches of doing nothing, "we have no way to think, reflect, heal, and sustain ourselves—individually or collectively," Odell writes. "There's a kind of nothing that's necessary for, at the end of the day, doing something."

Rested people also have greater cognitive flexibility, meaning they think more nimbly and respond better to changing demands than their always-on counterparts. The better rested you are, the more likely you are to find life meaningful and satisfying. And the clearer you are about the larger purpose you're working toward, the more motivated you'll feel on a day-to-day basis.

In the long run, the most fulfilled people are those psychologist Erik Erikson calls "generative," who focus on making lasting contributions rather than racking up individual wins. Though generative people work, sometimes intensely, the fruits of their work are directed outward and they understand the value of periodic retreat—not just to top up their energy reserves but also to evaluate where they're headed and why. Theirs is not the ethos of Aesop's ants, who toiled endlessly and hoarded the surplus resources they'd gathered.

How to set a work-and-rest rhythm that fuels generativity, though, is itself a matter of debate. Some trending self-care tactics, though well intended, are as extreme and impractical as workaholism itself. Not everyone wants to "quiet quit"—to disengage from work in all but name—or to sign up for retreats and wait for life-altering insights to descend.

Setting a pace that allows you to flourish is more of a fluid art, harder to hashtag or pin down. It demands a frank initial assessment of where win-centered definitions of success have led you, and what sustaining possibilities might arise if you choose pursuits with value that outweighs any praise they might garner.

Stuck in the Weeds of Doing

For insight into setting this elusive rhythm, I schedule some calls with Dr. Amy Baltzell, a former Olympic rower and sports psychologist who for more than two decades has been helping people pace themselves. On our first call, Baltzell zooms in to the heart of the matter: "If you had a magic wand and you could use it," she asks me, "what would you change?"

I pause. In recent years, I've taken on more work that feels meaningful—telling stories that help people understand themselves and tap into their own capacities—because I feel more motivated and energized when I do so. Having this focus has helped me pace myself, since I'm saving time and energy I used to spend chasing unrelated rabbit trails.

Even so, in stressed moments, I sometimes find myself reverting to overachiever mode, blitzing through a string of flashy but hollow assignments. Habits laid down more than three decades ago, it turns out, die hard—and it's this old programming I most want to banish. It doesn't help that individual wins can seem like the only attainable bright spots amid broad social and cultural dysfunction. "I was raised to work, keep moving, and if I wasn't doing that on a day-to-day basis, something was wrong," I tell Baltzell.

Baltzell explains that moving at full speed without a well-defined destination—what she calls getting "caught up in the weeds of doing"—is common among perennial strivers, and that the stakes of such aimless exertion are higher than most people realize. Driving yourself all out without sufficient reflection or recovery, Baltzell says, is like dieting intensely to improve your race times: It seems like a smart tactic at first, and then it abruptly backfires. "The thinner you get, the faster you go, the thinner you get, the faster you go. And then pretty soon, physiologically, there is a significant crash, and it's really hard to get back up to normal speed."

Recovering from such a crash is its own kind of white-knuckle challenge, as burnout researchers like Christina Maslach know. In a study of more than two hundred people treated for "stress-related exhaustion," more than 30 percent remained clinically exhausted a full seven years after their initial treatment, and only about 16 percent reported making a complete recovery. Insistence on forging ahead at all costs can bring you lower than you ever thought possible.

The promise of sustainable pacing is that it can help you steer clear of crashes like this before they happen. But because this approach feels alien when you're socialized into an always-on, win-obsessed culture, it helps to ease yourself in gradually.

Before trying to shift your existing rhythms, reflect on the pace you've kept much of your life and why. When you were growing up, what messages did you hear about the relative importance of work and rest? How did the culture around you shape your sense of how hard you ought to push yourself and what goals you ought to chase? And when you pursued the goals you felt you should, rather than those that felt more organic and purposeful, did you notice shifts in your energy or motivation levels?

Next, consider how your existing ideas about pacing have shaped your life's trajectory so far. If you've felt compelled to go all out toward a goal, how did it go? Did pushing yourself to the edge energize or deplete you? And if you've taken significant time off from work or other commitments, did that retreat leave you feeling bored and aimless, or restored and hungry to contribute?

These questions may not have predictable or straightforward answers. You may conclude that pushing your limits focuses and excites you—up until the umbrella threatens to flip inside out. You may realize that taking a week off feels so awkward you can't relax until the final few days, or that what most energizes you is only vaguely related to what you do daily. No matter what insights arise, reflecting on the results of past pacing decisions primes you to make future decisions that better serve you, helps you resolve any reflexive discomfort with the prospect of slowing down, and encourages you to develop a clearer sense of what an examined, well-paced life might look like.

The American dream of winning, and the zeal with which we pursue it, has always seemed like part of Max Weber's "unalterable order of things." But setting a measured pace—one that staves off exhaustion and promotes long-term flourishing—requires a willingness to alter that sacred order; it's a reckoning with the accumulated damage of endless striving. Pacing shifts demand a full inventory of what gets trampled underfoot at default speed.

Chapter 2

A Biological Reckoning

The oldest daughter of Indian immigrant parents, Patty Johnson had always been expected to do it all effortlessly. For years, she seemed to succeed with flying colors. In addition to excelling in school, she took on multiple household duties, mowing the lawn in the summer and shoveling the walk in winter.

But when Johnson enrolled in a doctoral program in psychology, her stress levels ratcheted still higher. Not only was she cramming at all hours to keep up with her intense workload, but she was also navigating a rocky marriage while raising two young daughters, who were often asking her to help out with their schoolwork. Though she felt she was perpetually running on empty, guilt seized her when she even considered letting up. When she thought about taking a few days to rest and recoup, the idea that she was selfish stopped her cold.

It wasn't long before the physical fallout of her grueling pace began to show up. "My body began to scream at me," Johnson says. She lost chunks of hair, exposing scattered bald patches the size of a quarter. Her head was also starting to throb more and more, a trend that escalated into ice pick headaches that hit each day at around four o'clock.

Johnson initially kept soldiering on, just as she had done for decades. "I refused to connect the physical symptoms with my stress," she says. "I told myself I could handle it all and do it well." When lab results showed her glucose levels and blood pressure were both elevated—indications she was starting to slide toward chronic illness—Johnson grew alarmed enough to face what was happening more squarely. If she didn't, she knew her next round of results might be worse.

But admitting that her default pace was no longer tenable went against all her ingrained programming. Like millions of perennial strivers, Johnson was accustomed to shunting her self-protective instincts aside in the service of some achievement or obligation that seemingly mattered more.

The progression from stress to chronic physical or mental illness, and even to early death, is now well documented, as predictable as gravity or aging itself. More insidiously, sustained stress can affect your daily choices in ways that steer you further away from long-term flourishing. When your body and mind feel as if they are under assault, it's only natural to focus on making it through the day. But people in survival mode can develop tunnel vision, which keeps them from making choices that fulfill them in the long run—and, as a result, their health and energy levels continue to plummet.

While a variety of events can trigger everyday stress, from job loss to illness to relationship conflicts, chronic stress sets in when there's a fundamental mismatch between your inner resources and what your environment demands of you. When you feel overextended on a regular basis—at work, in community life, or in relationships—skillful pacing shifts can help you regain a healthy equilibrium, the kind of balance that allows for ongoing flourishing.

The first step toward finding this equilibrium is figuring out how far you've strayed from it. To that end, basic medical testing can begin to show the physical and mental toll that stress has taken on you. Along with insights from doctors and therapists, this testing can help clarify what living at default speed has cost you, existentially as well as physically—and what you stand to gain by reassessing your pace.

A Perilous Cascade

As unmooring as the stress response can feel, it initially evolved to keep us alive. When we needed to respond to a life-or-death crisis, whether a savanna tiger in hot pursuit or a rival bent on revenge, the brain signaled the adrenal glands to dump a potent cocktail of stress hormones into the bloodstream. One major player here is adrenaline, which causes the heart rate to speed up, pushing more blood (and with it, energy) to every major organ. Another is cortisol, which cranks the nervous system into overdrive, sending the body into a high-alert state.

In the short term, this biological cascade is adaptive, allowing you to respond decisively in times of danger. But when conditions that drive stress persist—say, when you've been working overtime without a break for weeks, or when your bills are mounting as safety nets are dwindling—the stress-response mechanism gets pushed far beyond its original purpose. The body then stays on indefinite alert, as though a predator were forever lurking in the shadows. Adrenaline and cortisol levels remain elevated, sending your blood pressure and muscle tension skyward.

Signs of the toll this state takes are subtle at first. "It starts out by impacting your sleep, your mood, and your attention," says neuroscientist David Rabin, who studies the fallout of prolonged stress. "People get foggy—they can't remember things as well. They start to feel more agitated, easily irritable, not able to bounce back from stress as quickly."

If stress persists for more than a few weeks, or if it becomes chronic, a biological domino-fall effect begins. "In a resource-depleted system," Rabin says, "the parts that are depleted start to become diseased or damaged."

That damage shows up in ways familiar to people in profit-driven, always-on cultures. Accumulation of arterial plaque, which can usher in blood clots and strokes. Autoimmune reactions that can shift the body into a chronically inflamed state. In one California State University survey of populations around the world, people who lived at a faster pace also had higher rates of death from coronary heart disease—a stark reminder of what's really at stake in the pacing game.

The health effects of Patty Johnson's grueling pace hit home the first time she got a migraine headache with a visual aura, a condition tied to higher risk of strokes. "I suddenly saw bright flashing lights that became more intense," she says. "I wasn't sure if I was losing my vision or hallucinating." Though she learned her condition wasn't immediately dangerous, the visual effects and the stress-related headaches continued, forcing her to miss events and family gatherings.

Veterans of early-life pressure like Johnson may be more vulnerable to developing stress-related health conditions later on. People who report significant stress in childhood or adolescence end up in poorer overall health by their thirties, and many show signs of progressing toward chronic disease. Minority-group members and lower-income workers feel these effects even more acutely. Not only do people of color report higher stress levels than the general population, for instance, but they're also at risk of developing chronic illnesses stemming from that persistent stress.

Then there's the daily psychological impact. When you're under stress for years, Rabin explains, your fear response can become dissociated from the impulse that caused it. When this occurs, your anxiety may spike drastically, no matter what's actually happening. Over time, this anxiety "grows bigger and bigger and bigger," Rabin says. "It eventually becomes a giant fear signal—we can't figure out where it's coming from."

As Rabin continues, I realize I know exactly what he means. When I've been pushing myself too hard, I sometimes bolt upright from sleep, my heart hammering as though I've barely evaded some predator in hot pursuit. What sets this panic apart from normal fear is that it's free-floating, not spurred on by specific thoughts about what's happening in my life. It's primordial, physiological—like an in-breath or eye blink.

Prolonged stress also interferes with the brain's executive function and with higher-order thought, as Ivanka Savic Berglund of Sweden's Karolinska Institute found when she scanned the brains of more than one hundred people, some of whom were under significant work stress. Compared to non-stressed participants, members of the stressed group had pronounced thinning in the prefrontal cortex, a brain area that governs complex thinking and decision-making.

People with more cortical thinning were also, on average, more psychologically brittle. They were less able to cope with negative emotions, and the fear-processing parts of their brain were larger, hinting they were primed to react more strongly to unusual events. Brain areas that detected threat had mushroomed, while those in charge of higher-order thought had atrophied.

When I touch base with my longtime psychiatrist, Sean Haugh, he warns that anyone with a history of mental health struggles needs to take special care to keep stress levels controlled. "As long as you do, you will manage whatever comes to your doorstep," he says. "But if you don't, it's almost impossible."

I press him about what happens if you don't ease back when warning signs appear. "Basic life functioning activities are going to be disturbed," he says. "Sleep, eating, thinking, concentrating." Haugh also points out that unaddressed stress affects the normal functioning of the midbrain, which governs sleep cycles, blood pressure, and heart rate—and that under those conditions, meeting your job's intellectual demands will become a Sisyphean task. Chronic mild stress is linked to a lower firing rate in certain neurons in the midbrain, which may lead to difficulty thinking your way around life's daily challenges.

"Our thinking brain is a dependent brain. It depends on the stability of the midbrain below," Haugh explains. "When the midbrain is wobbly, the thinking brain—no matter how intelligent a super-brain you have— is not going to function." Ironically, then, in attempting to squeeze the most out of your talents, you can undermine the mental architecture that allowed those talents to develop in the first place.

Not only does chronic stress impede clear thinking, it can also rob you of the ability to find life fulfilling. To flourish, people need to have a sense that they are contributing to the world in a concrete way. It stands to reason, then, that prolonged stress inhibits flourishing; it's hard to contribute meaningfully when your body and mind feel under assault. (Crucially, it isn't the number of hours you work that predicts a decrease in flourishing. Instead, it's the amount of stress you're under—your sense that the demands you face exceed your available resources.)

The fallout intensifies when full-scale burnout hits. Burned-out people have less robust immune defenses, picking up infections more easily. They also, cruelly, may have trouble getting much sleep at all, since stress hormones throw bodily systems that govern their sleep/wake cycles out of whack. The very rest they need for renewal eludes them.

This kind of degradation isn't unique to humans; it's common throughout the animal kingdom. When prolonged heat exposure stresses corals—those microscopic sea creatures that grow into living ramparts— they expel the green algae living inside them, which serves as their main food source. Without this sustenance, they starve or succumb to disease. What makes us think we can be exceptions to the rule?

Gauging Your Body's Resilience

When I reach out to David Rabin for a primer on assessing stress's mounting health effects, he tells me the process is simpler than many people assume. Theoretically, he says, you can go through an exhaustive medical workup and come away with a personalized profile—a detailed analysis of how well you're handling stress, physically and mentally.

But for most people, in-office scans and profiles are likely overkill. You don't need a lot of fancy technology to assess your baseline stress levels, Rabin says. Instead, he recommends tracking heart rate variability (HRV), a measure of how much time elapses between each of your heartbeats and how much that interval changes over time.

HRV, which you can measure daily with a device like a chest strap or Oura ring, is "one of our most reliable measures of resilience in the body, or how recovered the body is," Rabin says. HRV data offer a window onto which part of your nervous system has the upper hand on any given day: the sympathetic one, which drives your heart rate up when you face threats, or the parasympathetic one, which eases you into a calmer state once threats have receded.

In general, the more your heart rate changes between beats, the better. That means your nervous system is quickly snapping back to a relaxed state after stressful moments. But if your heart rate is less variable, your threat response may be persisting longer than it needs to, making you vulnerable to stress-related ill effects. Because people's natural HRV "set points" can vary, having an HRV reading that's higher than someone else's isn't necessarily cause for alarm. What's important is establishing your own HRV baseline through repeated readings and observing how what happens in your life affects that baseline.

At Rabin's suggestion, I head online and order a chest electrode strap, a simple device that sends heart rate data to my smartphone. Feeling self-conscious, I breathe in and out for two minutes while the sensor records my heartbeats. Then I hold my breath, waiting for my phone screen to flash the verdict.

"Your sympathetic activity appears to be abnormally elevated," the pop-up message blinks back. Repeated readings confirm that my nervous system stays on high alert for extended intervals, a tendency that research shows can stem from prolonged stress. The term "high-strung" has direct resonance for me: When I'm under stress, self-imposed or external, I feel like a violin string that's been pulled too tight. "If I had to describe your autonomic nervous system, it's much more like a Maserati than a Volkswagen," the psychiatrist Joseph Arpaia says after looking at my HRV data. "It revs. You touch the gas, and boom!"

By taking an HRV reading regularly—once a day, or a few times a week—you can get a better idea of what your current stress baseline is, as well as how events in your life affect your readings. While a single low reading isn't necessarily cause for concern, a string of them over a week or so hints at the kind of entrenched stress that triggers physical and mental upset. When you start to see that your HRV is trending downward over time, David Rabin explains, it's a sign that your stress is likely taking a long-term toll on your body and mind.

Hormonal Disturbance

Cortisol testing has emerged as another promising way to gauge how much stress your body is under. An essential hormone, cortisol plays a role in setting the body's inner clock when, in the hours before awakening, the pituitary gland signals the adrenal glands to start churning it out.

Though cortisol is often dubbed "the stress hormone," the concentrated burst the body supplies before you wake up is a healthy response: It ensures that you'll feel alert enough to tackle the day.

In chronically stressful conditions, however, this normal response is thrown off kilter. The cortisol awakening burst may ascend to dangerous heights, causing more jitters than you'd normally feel and contributing to free-floating anxiety. Other times, cortisol rises at times of the day when it would normally recede. Studies show that prolonged stress is tied to a variety of abnormal cortisol-release patterns.

Your doctor can order a cortisol test for you, but if you prefer, you can initiate the process yourself. Since hormones remain present in blood and saliva samples for several days, you can order some kinds of tests online, complete them at home, and mail your samples back to the issuing lab. The kinds of tests available range from one-time morning cortisol measurements to tests involving multiple samples, which closely assess how your levels change from morning to evening. Your health insurance may be more likely to cover cortisol testing that your doctor orders, but you can often purchase at-home tests using a flexible spending account (FSA) or health savings account (HSA).

To complete the cortisol test I order, I need to spit into six different tubes—the first one as soon as I get up, another two tubes thirty minutes and an hour later, and the remaining three tubes in the afternoon and evening. I seal the saliva-filled tubes in a frantic state. I'm about to leave for a weeklong trip, and mailing off the tubes is one of the zillion things I need to check off my list before I go.

About a week later, I hear back from the test company. My cortisol levels do look somewhat wonky, just not in the way I'd suspected. I'd assumed my periodic 4:00 a.m. jitters meant my cortisol would be through the roof when I got up, but my awakening cortisol rise turned out to be fairly normal. As the day wore on, however, it was a different story. Though my cortisol dropped to normal range at about noon, it rose abruptly in the evening and remained high until around bedtime.

"Our cortisol is supposed to go up in the morning, and then taper off during the day and is kind of low at nighttime when it's time to go to sleep," the pharmacist says when I call. "What this looks like is an evening cortisol rise, which is going to make it difficult to fall asleep."

In isolation, cortisol testing might or might not be meaningful. What's important is how it fits into the overall picture. My test represents a snapshot of one day in my life—and it's possible that my evening cortisol levels were high because I was scrambling to prepare for my trip. On the other hand, I often do have trouble winding down for the night, just as my test results would suggest, leading to morning exhaustion that makes it hard to push through the day.

For Massachusetts interior designer Hannah Oravec, hormone testing supplied evidence of the physical toll her work stress was starting to take. Oravec was trying to get her own design business off the ground while working a full-time job, resulting in a schedule that would exhaust many Olympic athletes. She'd wake up at 4:00 a.m., work on her business for a few hours, and head to her full-time job, where she regularly put in ten-plus-hour days. Since she loved designing, her passion initially seemed to carry her through. "I made excuses to not really do much besides work," she says.

It wasn't until Oravec and her husband decided to start a family that she tuned more closely into her body's distress signals. She'd noticed that her menstrual cycles were getting irregular, which she knew might make pregnancy hard to achieve, so she went in for a panel of hormone tests to assess what was happening.

When the test results came back, Oravec's doctor explained that—among other things—her cortisol had been elevated for so long that her levels finally crashed owing to her body's depleted state. That helped explain her chronic exhaustion, as well as her menstrual irregularities. "My hormones were all over the place. That caused my body to shut down its reproductive cycle," she says. "It was a huge wakeup call for me." If she wanted to have a family, she realized, she'd have to set a different pace, one that would allow her to thrive in every sense.

Assessing Your Burnout Risk

For a bird's-eye view of how your pace is affecting your health and outlook, you can also take the Maslach Burnout Inventory. Developed by Berkeley psychologist and burnout expert Christina Maslach, it's considered the gold standard of burnout assessments, and it's offered as a self-test, as well as a clinical-assessment tool. It contains a list of statements like "I feel like I'm at the end of my rope" and "I feel tired when I get up in the morning and have to face another day at work," and you're asked to decide how much you agree with each statement, indicated on a scale of 0 to 6.

The test is designed to give you a clearer sense of how close you're getting to a physical and psychological crash—and, if you're there already, how dire your situation is so you can determine what you need to do in response. When I take the test, it takes me about twenty minutes to work my way through the series of twenty-two questions. Though I'm somewhat relieved to learn I'm at low to moderate risk of burnout, I know I may need to revisit the test as conditions in my work and life shift.

High scores on this test are often the carryover of longtime pacing problems that have gone unaddressed, and they're also a harbinger of potential future breakdown. People who meet the criteria for burnout, studies show, are about twice as likely to develop heart disease or type 2 diabetes than people who score in a normal range.

Bursts of intense work that aren't followed by planned downtime, Maslach warns, are not physically or psychologically sustainable. "If you really go all out, as any good athlete will tell you, you've got to recover after that sprint in order to get back up and be able to do it again. Every day, all the time, you cannot be operating at that sprint pace."

An Honest Reckoning

Many of us have known for years about the tradeoffs between health and typical Western work rhythms. We've read the studies showing that people who go all out on a regular basis have higher rates of heart disease and early death. But much of that can feel theoretical, as distant and detached as a research paper summary.

If there's anything concrete that comes out of assessing stress's effects on your body and mind, it's that the sense of detachment fades. It's one thing to suspect, vaguely, that your current pace is wearing you down, existentially as well as physically. It's quite another thing to confront more direct evidence—tests that show you have disturbed sleep cycles, an overactive nervous system, and hormone swings that impede your daily functioning. Evidence like this helps motivate you to correct the commonest of all pacing errors: going full steam ahead, per cultural dictates, heedless of the longer-term consequences.

It's crucial, however, to put your test results into context. If you seek out any stress-related assessments on your own, make sure to discuss the results with medical providers or therapists you trust. Not only can providers help you interpret the meaning of a particular result, they can also draw on your medical history to recommend further relevant testing, giving you a clearer picture of how your current pace affects your health.

Even with a mountain of evidence that your pace is too grueling, you might conclude you have no choice but to keep going if you want to retain your job and support those you love. But the notion that dialing back means sacrificing what's most essential is false, argues executive coach and Brown University consultant Daryl Appleton.

Study after study shows that trimming work hours by 10 percent or more *improves* your performance, rather than degrading it. And if your pace—at work or elsewhere—is driving you toward stress-induced illness, your physical and mental decline will steadily undermine the contributions you most want to make, in the lives of those you love as well as in the wider world. "Not to be flexible and malleable," Appleton says, "is going to cause you to break. That is going to be the number one thing that holds you back."

A Deliberate Reset

Recalibrating your pace, using the research-backed strategies this book explores, is a highly individual process based on understanding and heeding your energetic limits, which may be completely different from someone else's. Pacing overhauls can feel destabilizing, since they go against the social programming that's been instilled from an early age. Yet it's possible to circumvent that programming and reverse health declines while doing what you need to do to support yourself and your family.

One way to begin titrating your pace is to reassess specific tasks and commitments that seem, on the surface, to be nonnegotiable. You may be used to tackling big projects alone, telling yourself no one else will do them justice, or plunging into endless text threads with team members who pepper you with two or three questions for every one you manage to answer. But by dialing down judiciously, like a runner who titrates her pace to three-quarters of full speed, you can maintain the basic contours of your life while making space to replenish your energy stores. Though you may opt for more radical pace and focus shifts later on, those shifts are best undertaken once you've brought your body and mind back into equilibrium.

For Hannah Oravec, incremental retreat proved the ideal approach. After Oravec received her alarming round of test results, she developed a plan with her doctor to pare back her hours and start logging full nights of sleep. By delegating some work duties to other employees, she was able to rest more while maintaining her design business. Her menstrual cycles returned, and she and her husband soon learned they were expecting their first child.

As Patty Johnson came to terms with her health challenges, she decided to make her own incremental pacing shifts. Though she continued to work full time toward her doctorate, she slashed the hours she spent tending to others out of obligation. She had her kids tackle more homework on their own, and she rebuffed relatives who were leaning hard on her for emotional support. "I drew lines with friends and family that only saw me as the healer," she says. At the same time, she went deeper into areas of her life that energized her. That included her studies—she was genuinely excited about becoming a therapist and helping clients—as well as hobbies and activities that she had put by the wayside.

"My girls and I colored and did teatime. I took long walks with my puppy, without rushing back to do homework," she says. "It all got done in the end, the things I had to do, and more importantly the things I wanted to do. I didn't do it perfectly, but I did it with peace." Her blood pressure and blood sugar levels began dropping and have since settled into a normal range.

A well-calibrated pace defies cultural directives to go all out, consequences be damned. It reestablishes a solid physical and mental baseline—one that gradually broadens your focus from mere survival to growth and contribution. If you've maintained a punishing pace for years and watched it shatter you for almost as long, it's time for a deeper reset.

Chapter 3

Plotting a Narrative Arc

Jony M. Weiss was no stranger to pushing herself to the limit. For years, she'd worked as a California public health educator while trying to care for her aging parents in New York—her mother had developed multiple sclerosis, while her father was battling dementia.

As her parents' health grew worse, Weiss kept on chugging. She flew back and forth across the country, juggling work, elder caregiving, and raising a family. When she was at home with her husband and son, her remote-care duties made it hard to relax—especially when her parents' morning calls roused her at 5:00 a.m. California time. And when she was with her parents, she worried about her son back in California. "I was trying to be sure, *Does he get his needs met?*" Those worries persisted when she started managing the remote caregiving process almost full time, giving up her steady job in the process.

After her parents passed away (and after she'd wound up their affairs, which was nearly a full-time job in itself), Weiss hoped to set a more sustainable pace in her post-caregiving years, one that would allow her to focus on what mattered most.

One day, Weiss stumbled on an article that caught her attention. Viewing life as a hero's journey, scientists reported, boosted people's sense of meaning and shaped the arc of their lives from that point forward. The lead researcher, Boston College management professor Ben Rogers, had created what he called a "re-storying" exercise, a series of writing prompts to help people retell their life stories in hero's journey terms. Rogers's research was still so new that the exercise wasn't yet available to the public, so Weiss emailed him to ask if he'd be willing to share it with her, in hopes it might help her direct her future steps.

Thoughtful pacing requires paring excess from a cluttered life, and personal storytelling can help further this streamlining purpose. Stories never recount everything that happened—at least, the best ones don't. They shape elements of what happened into a narrative with a clear beginning, middle, and end, making sense of events that might otherwise seem chaotic and disconnected. They bring what's essential to the foreground so the inessential can recede.

Done properly, reflective storytelling underscores what gives you purpose and defines your place as contributor to a larger whole, setting you up for long-term flourishing. "One of the primary ways that we find meaning and make meaning in our lives is the stories that we tell, both to ourselves and to other people," Rogers says.

For millions who hustle on a daily basis, life feels arduous because—however fine-tuned their time-blocking skills—their days contain little in which they feel invested, an existential problem no time-management fix can address. Re-storying directly addresses the deficit of purpose that plagues overachiever culture. The clarity to be found in re-storying, the sharpened sense of what you want to hurl yourself toward and why, allows you to set a pace that's more energizing than draining.

Most people, like distance runners, focus best and feel most motivated when they have a distinct purpose or goal in mind—one they formulate based on their own values, not one dictated by win-at-all-costs imperatives. The meaning re-storying supplies can guide the day-to-day cadence of your life and the projects you take on, whether or not they're related to your job. And in revealing what's most essential to you, the re-storying process helps clarify what you can set aside, opening up room for rest and contemplation even as you focus more intently on what matters most.

The Power of Story

From epic poets onward, storytellers have understood their art's clarifying function, the way stories boil events down to their essence and underscore what's most vital. The author Milan Kundera recognized the human desire to locate themes in life that shape everything that follows. Such anchoring themes—say, the transformative power of love or the need to rescue someone in trouble—help people structure their lives around a larger purpose no matter what happens to them.

Among the first researchers to examine the importance of this personal meaning-making was the psychologist Victor Frankl. After the Nazis sent Frankl to the Auschwitz concentration camp during World War II, he realized that without a clear sense of why he wanted to live on, he would meet the same fate as those dying all around him. He came to see his life as a quest for two things: to reunite with his wife, and to rewrite a research manuscript the Nazis had destroyed. Buoyed by his ongoing love for his wife and his scientific goals, Frankl managed to survive against all odds, in large part because he focused on what he wanted his life to be about regardless of his imprisonment. Amid beatings and deprivation, "my mind clung to my wife's image, imagining it with an uncanny acuteness," Frankl wrote. "I heard her answering me, saw her smile, her frank and encouraging look."

Frankl's imprisonment showed him the galvanizing effect of having a higher purpose in dire circumstances. The story he'd told himself at Auschwitz about what mattered most to him, he realized, had saved his life. He went on to develop a new treatment approach he called logotherapy, designed to help depressed and listless clients connect to sources of meaning in their own lives.

Later research showed how certain kinds of personal storytelling helped people clarify their purpose—and also spurred their desire to act on it. Psychologists Brady Jones and Dan McAdams asked people to tell a story with their own agency and abilities at the center, about a time they'd set a particular goal and made it happen, say, or a time they fell short of a goal and learned something valuable as a result.

After participants told these kinds of stories about themselves, they scored higher in measures of persistence weeks later and got better grades in school than members of a control group. In reflecting on how they'd faced obstacles while chasing important goals, people seemed to gain clarity not just about what meant most to them, but about what goals best suited them.

Some of my conversations with Amy Baltzell have felt like early attempts to distill this kind of meaning. At one point, Baltzell challenges me to come up with some kind of touchstone I can return to when the world seems to be going to hell. "What's going to help you tolerate these feelings and thoughts, and then put your attention on what you truly care about, instead of being pulled down? In those dark moments, what can you bring to mind?"

"I've been writing since I was five or six years old," I say, pausing to collect my thoughts. "At the heart of it, there was just this love of communicating, bringing something to somebody that would help them not feel so alone."

Baltzell asks me to put this idea on an index card, and what I end up writing down—the theme of my narrative, so to speak—reads a bit like a shopping list: "light, truth, helping people not feel alone."

"Put it someplace where you can see it," Baltzell says. "Put it someplace where it's reminding you."

The Hero's Journey Archetype

I put the index card I filled out on my desk, and at times, it does seem to help me keep my larger goals front of mind. Yet there's also something that feels incomplete about "light, truth, helping people not feel alone" on its own. It's true that I want to help clarify things that seem confusing. But the snippets I've written down seem to exist in a bubble, with no connection to the past or future.

My sense of disconnection wouldn't surprise Ben Rogers. He's spent years studying the role more complete life narratives can play in helping people understand not just what matters to them but also how that guiding focus emerged in the first place. Narratives "connect certain elements. They go, 'That thing I did five years ago led me to who I am today,'" Rogers says. "That's the power of the way we tell our stories."

Rogers has long understood, though, that certain modes of personal storytelling are better than others at revealing themes that animate people's lives, especially the story structure called the "hero's journey." Sometimes known as a "monomyth," a hero's journey story features a character who sets out on an adventure, triumphs over obstacles along the way, and comes back transformed, bringing something valuable back to the community. Classic stories from around the world, from Homer's *Odyssey* to the Mesopotamian Epic of Gilgamesh, closely follow this basic template.

Rogers suspected that hero's journey–style storytelling might be a powerful vehicle for helping people understand their experiences and clarify their ultimate goals. Other scientists had found that people who told epic-style stories about themselves often led lives that were rich in meaning and contribution. What no one had quite figured out, though, was which way the causality ran. Was epic storytelling actually propelling people toward more meaningful, engaged lives, or were thriving people simply more likely to tell life stories that resembled the hero's journey?

To find out, Rogers and his colleagues enrolled hundreds of people in a re-storying exercise in which they rewrote their own life stories to parallel the phases of the classic hero's journey. The study's version of the hero's journey involved several basic elements, including a shift that drives protagonists to set an important goal; the onset of challenges as they pursue that goal; personal growth or transformation along the journey; enlisting allies along the way; and a triumphant return with some insight or contribution that serves the community.

After people completed this exercise, they reported that they found their lives more meaningful than they had beforehand, while control participants, who simply wrote about different aspects of their lives, did not report this change. That suggested that the re-storying exercise was indeed responsible for the meaning boost.

Rogers's most striking finding, though, wasn't just that the exercise helped people find meaning. It was that this deeper meaning influenced the everyday choices people made in challenging moments.

At one point, Rogers asked people in his re-storying trial how they planned to handle a major problem in their lives. Those who had completed the re-storying process were more likely to say they would look for direct ways to address the issue—say, by speaking to a supervisor to resolve a conflict, rather than remaining passive. They also looked at the problem itself more positively, seeing it as a chance to learn and correct course just as seasoned pacers do.

The clarifying function of the re-storying process seems to bolster focus and resolve in the face of challenge. These traits are integral to a well-paced life, helping you channel your energy in directions that will strengthen and fulfill you. And when you want to restore the focus re-storying supplies, you can revisit or repeat the process, integrating the insights you gain into your overall mindset.

Despite re-storying's benefits, Rogers sometimes gets an incredulous response when he makes his case for hero's journey re-storying outside the academic world. Most people don't picture themselves as heroes—after all, they haven't made news headlines or rescued anyone from a burning building. "People in our studies were, like, 'I'm not sure I can see myself in that way,'" Rogers says.

But they begin to buy into it more when he explains that re-storying isn't about picturing yourself as superhuman; it's about casting yourself as the protagonist of a larger narrative. "People have new experiences all the time, they face challenges, they grow from them. These things that you may think are outside of your realm are actually things that you have in your life."

One Chapter at a Time

After Jony Weiss wrote to Ben Rogers, she found a message from him in her inbox a few days later. He hadn't yet created a DIY version of the re-storying process that anyone could try, he said. But thanks to Weiss, who'd contacted him in search of such a process, he planned to create one over the summer and offer it in a quiz-like format on his website.

When Rogers's site launched in mid-2024, he sent Weiss the link and she jumped in. Rogers and his team, she saw, had boiled down the re-storying process to eight basic writing prompts.

How to Write Your Own Hero's Journey

If you want to clarify what brings meaning and purpose to your life, you can try the re-storying process Rogers developed for his study participants. Here are the eight prompts Rogers uses to give people a framework for describing their own hero's journey.

Protagonist: What makes you you? Think about your identity, personality, and core values.

Shift: What change of setting or novel experience prompted your journey to become who you are today? (What was your call to adventure?)

Quest: What overall goal were you striving for that led to who you are today?

Challenge: What challenges or obstacles, such as a nemesis/rival or negative event, stood in the way of your journey?

Allies: Who supported or helped you in your journey?

Transformation: How did you personally grow as part of your journey to become who you are today?

Legacy: In what ways has your journey left a legacy?

Integration: Reflecting on the various aspects of yourself and your story, describe how you might see yourself as a hero on an epic journey.

The first prompt asks how you see yourself as a protagonist in your life: "What makes you *you*? Think about your identity, personality and core values."

The next few steps invite you to consider how events in your life parallel specific stages of the hero's journey. The "shift" prompt, "What change of setting or novel experience prompted your journey to become who you are today?" evokes the "call to adventure" events seen in many classic stories. Other prompts ask you to describe what quest you see yourself on and how it has unfolded: what overall goal you were striving for that led to who you are; what challenges stood in your way; and which allies helped you along the way.

At the crux of the re-storying process, tellers locate moments of transformation: "How did you personally grow as part of your journey to become who you are today?" The final prompts ask you what legacy you've been able to leave to others and how you see yourself as a hero on an epic journey.

Weiss was eager to explore the broader significance of challenges that had stretched her to the limit, so she knew she wanted to approach the re-storying process slowly and deliberately. For the "protagonist" question, which asked her to reflect on her identity and values, she took at least ten minutes to think before starting to write. She jotted down a few sentences about her desire to support other people's health and happiness—a theme that had helped inspire her career in public health.

What stood out to Weiss, as she worked her way through the prompts, was that considering each phase of the journey separately made what could have been an onerous process feel approachable, not overwhelming. "I was like, 'Oh, all I have to do is a little bit at a time.'"

After addressing the early prompts, Weiss arrived at the prompt that addressed the major challenge that had defined her life for years. During her prime working years, as others around her pursued straightforward career paths, her struggle to care for her aging parents had defined her. It had all started when she found out her parents were forgetting to pay their rent, taxes, and apartment cleaners. "I realized, as things deteriorated more and more, that I needed to get more and more involved," she says.

As her parents' health issues grew worse, Weiss toured several care facilities in New York and California. She also spoke with her father's geriatrician, who mentioned that, given his condition, her father would feel disoriented if he were not at home. After she concluded that no facility could serve both her parents adequately, Weiss made the difficult decision to scale back her career so she could become her parents' full-time care manager. She threw herself full tilt into her new role, arranging for an around-the-clock series of specialists and caregivers, and even hiring an art therapist for her mother, who was an abstract painter, so she could continue to have a creative outlet.

While Weiss adjusted to the demands of her new role, she struggled with feeling she was never doing enough. When she was with her parents, she couldn't be with the rest of her family, and vice versa—a nonnegotiable, frustrating reality. And to care for her parents, she had to dial back the public health work she loved doing and reject the pervasive messaging that her career achievements determined her worth.

As Weiss recalled the pacing challenges she'd faced, following the story prompts helped her remember what—and who—had kept her on what she'd instinctively felt was the right path. In responding to Rogers's "allies" prompt, Weiss felt buoyed in thinking about the network of helpers she'd assembled, from an expert in elder law to friends who offered to attend appointments with her. One friend she'd grown up with offered her a place to stay every time she was in New York. Another friend, a nurse, helped talk her through how to manage her parents' healthcare, and she found an excellent care manager who remained on site with her parents when she couldn't be there. "I thought, 'Look how many people are involved,'" Weiss says. "You never know where your allies may be."

Weiss knew not everyone would have made the same choices she did, especially since her parents ended up needing care for close to a decade before their death. As she reflected on what transformation had come out of this challenge, though, she realized that her choices had allowed her to live out one of her most important values: doing the very best she could for loved ones. That choice had made her life feel meaningful even when it was logistically hard to manage. "We want to pursue happiness," she says, "but maybe something's more important than the feeling of happiness. Doing the right thing by my parents became more important." That realization cemented her belief that, going forward, she wanted to help others through their worst moments, even if it was hard or inconvenient—a conviction that would inform her plans in the years ahead, streamlining the possibilities in front of her.

How Story Informs Pacing

When you recast your life in hero's journey terms, you start to recognize echoes of what others have confronted for all of time. "The things that tormented me most," novelist James Baldwin told an interviewer, "were the very things that connected me with all the people who were alive, who had ever been alive." And by highlighting the values and actions that mean most to you, the re-storying process helps clarify what goals you want to pace yourself toward, lending energy and direction to your day-to-day plans.

Research confirms that a broadly meaningful goal or purpose, the kind reflective storytelling encourages, can motivate you to take specific action to fulfill those aims. In a Texas A&M study, people who thought about the larger significance of their goals—for example, wanting to get good grades so they could pursue helping careers—were more inspired to meet those goals than people who had no such broader purpose in mind.

The motivation you gain through re-storying can help dictate the tone and pace you set in the years that follow, ultimately altering your daily rhythms. In the final phases of the re-storying process, Jony Weiss considered the legacy she wanted to leave others, something that would persist long after she'd gone. She decided she wanted part of that legacy to be passing on the knowledge she had gained in caring for her parents. That insight has energized her as she delves into a developing project: a book about how to manage caregiving and legal matters for older relatives while preserving your own mental health. "So many people said, 'Could you hurry up and write this?'" she says. She also regularly counsels friends and family members who face challenges with aging relatives.

This kind of purposeful focus can affect not just the pace you set in your work but also how you respond to setbacks and trials. Workers motivated to fulfill a higher purpose, research shows, are better able to handle periodic stress at work than their less motivated counterparts. Clearly defined purpose, then, can serve as a hedge against burnout, giving you resilience to steer through challenging times.

My own re-storying process helps me get more specific about what adds most meaning to my life—and to recalibrate my pace in response. The biggest catalyst is the prompt that asks me to describe how I overcame core challenges, from struggles with depression to an abuse crisis that emerged at my old school. As I reflect, I realize I've often responded to shameful, painful, or ignored truths by describing them as best I could, documenting them to help others understand them precisely.

What I want, I'm seeing, isn't just to help people feel less alone. I want to describe things people know or sense on a deep level but may not be able to articulate. I want to sharpen their awareness of what's happening so they can better assess how to respond. I want to supply the kind of raw material that fuels necessary upheaval.

This recognition has helped guide me toward the kind of work that clarifies difficult realities and has made it easier to turn down the work that doesn't. Doing this has lifted a source of self-imposed drag I hadn't acknowledged—and eliminating that drag has cleared time and mental space for reading, thinking, and recharging. And the tough days, the ones when I have to work late on deadline or interview someone who's been through hell, don't seem as exhausting when I think about the upheaval they can help create.

I jot something new on the back of the index card I made with Baltzell, a quote I remembered from a Claire Vaye Watkins essay. "Let us name those things that are nameless," Watkins wrote. "Let us use our words and our gazes to make the invisible visible." When I return to Watkins's essay, another passage jumps out at me. "Let us hear the stories we are telling ourselves about ourselves. Let us remember that we become the stories we tell."

Re-Storying Redux

The stories we tell about ourselves can, in fact, be quite sticky. When researchers at New York University asked people to tell the story of their life, then asked them to do it again four years later, they found that the stories remained mostly the same from the first telling to the second. That suggests that if your autobiographical narrative has positive components, such as overcoming significant obstacles, you may reap the motivational benefits of that narrative for years after you piece it together.

But while the stories that define your life will always be a sustaining framework, their influence can recede somewhat amid kid drop-offs, work emergencies, and mountains of paperwork. "Life gets very complicated, very quickly," Ben Rogers concedes.

To offset this kind of fadeout, Rogers is experimenting with ways to help people keep core narrative elements front of mind. One effective strategy, he says, is to talk with people you know well about the direction and goals your narration has uncovered, perhaps a few times a year, or any time you want to revisit what you gained in the re-storying process.

Not only do these conversations help reinforce key elements of your story but they also allow you to tweak or revisit it, if you choose, drawing on feedback from those you trust. Rogers suspects that this social process helps solidify and deepen the impact of re-storying, so that the insights it supplies become more integral to how you see the world and plan your days. "That's the research that we want to build on," he says. "What are the ways that telling this story to others might create this feedback loop, such that you're not having to do this writing exercise every day to feel these benefits?"

In addition to seeking social feedback, you can repeat the re-storying process every so often, in part to prevent the extended reign of narratives that no longer fit. There's something too essentializing, something almost dangerous, about a narrative that bleeds over into testimonial—the kind that's been repeated or rehearsed so many times you know almost every word by heart. Though it can promote focus, it can also become constraining, closing off possibilities outside its own well-defined arc.

In epics and fairy tales, "they lived happily ever after" is either stated or implied. But Rogers's guiding narratives feature quests that are open-ended, with space for what's essential to morph and fluctuate. "If you have a change in your life, you have to incorporate that into your new story," Rogers says. "Anything can be looked at—the good thing, the bad thing, the complicated thing."

Repeating the narrative-mapping process can add surprising richness to your initial re-storying efforts. The more pivotal journeys you look back on, the more surprising parallels you start to recognize between them, while narrating each one may help you understand aspects of the others you hadn't considered.

The ideal way to revisit the re-storying process depends on what you hope to gain from it. "If you need perspective in one life domain, focus on just that," Rogers says. "To gain some general perspective, think of your overall life as a hero's journey."

• • •

The clarity that comes from Rogers's process may expand your sense of possibility in ways that feel intimidating. While it's motivating to locate precisely what brings meaning to your life, doing so also underscores the grit you'll need to realize that meaning. At the same time, the way guiding narratives help you decide what to embrace and what to set aside is freeing, allowing you to think and plan and recover between stretches of focused effort.

For Jony Weiss, the hero's journey narration offered closure on one of her most difficult chapters, which helped give her the mental freedom to set a less harried pace. Succinctly describing what she went through, she says, has helped her glean meaning from that episode of her story without feeling immersed in it any longer. "I grew from it, and I have more skills, more knowledge, more wisdom. For myself, for the people who know me, for other people I influence." That realization has fueled her as she tackles her book project and other plans to support overworked caregivers.

When I return to the index card I finished after re-storying—the one that reads "light, truth, helping people not feel alone" on one side and "let us name those things that are nameless" on the other side—it points me back to my own sharpened sense of where I'm headed. Though the narrative arc I've outlined remains open-ended, locating it has helped me set new, more sustaining rhythms.

Chapter 4

Find Your Pulse

It's an unusually warm day in May, and Ajeé Wilson is circling the track at Maguire Stadium in the Chestnut Hill neighborhood of Philadelphia, Pennsylvania. Save for a single unbothered walker, no one's on the track or in the stands, and that's the way Wilson likes it. Though she's been at the top of her sport for more than a decade, winning the 800-meter event at the 2022 World Indoor Championships and making it to the Tokyo Olympics, she trains best when she concentrates on her own agenda—not on whoever might be watching.

During her training season, Wilson's daily routine follows a comfortable rhythm, alternating focused stints of effort with periods of rest. After she eats breakfast and starts to feel alert, usually a little before 10:00 a.m., she heads over to Maguire, where she launches into her training plan—a series of sprints and longer endurance runs, sandwiched between stints of downtime to let her body and mind recover.

Wilson has mastered the art of pacing on multiple levels. As a specialist in the 800-meter, which occupies a middle ground between sprints and distance races, she balances a sprinter's instinct to go all out with a marathoner's keen sense of when to hold back. And as an athlete invested in extending her decade-plus career, she has designed a daily routine that syncs with her energy peaks and valleys throughout the day. She tackles her most intense training in late morning, when she's most apt to be alert and focused. When her energy levels bottom out, she does a 180-degree shift, committing just as strongly to rest as she does to training.

This strategic "pulsing," working with the body's and mind's natural rhythms, defies a cultural narrative we rarely question: that we can exert maximum effort on command through sheer willpower, and that this exertion ought to be celebrated. "We socially praise struggle," Wilson reflects. "We like the champions who had to work through something. Otherwise, when you achieve what you want, it's not going to taste good, or it's not going to be as noteworthy."

Despite her world-class achievements, Wilson has never relished struggle for its own sake, in part because she's learned it often predicts a coming crash. Instead, she approaches her training with what she calls "rigid flexibility," akin to trauma expert Gabor Maté's concept of "response flexibility." She considers each move she makes and ensures her actions align with her long-term intentions, and she shifts course—sometimes on the fly—if they do not. Though Wilson commits to reaching specific running goals each day, she builds plenty of give into her schedule, allowing her to maintain the energy and motivation she needs to make it through the season.

On and off the track, a pulsed work pace that follows natural energy highs and lows allows you to flourish while pursuing the goals that matter most to you. In the long run, this cyclical, responsive self-awareness will sustain you far longer than trying to override your own biology. We must "learn to live our own lives as a series of sprints," writes performance psychologist Jim Loehr, "fully engaging for periods of time, and then fully disengaging and seeking renewal before jumping back into the fray."

Rather than toiling in set, self-defeating ways, you can master the art of periodic retreat, backing off when your energy dwindles and going full throttle again once it's topped up. "When we think of professional sports, we think of very rigid programming and planning. I prefer a schedule that's more fluid," Wilson says. "I know what my days look like, but I also know where I can wiggle and do what I need to."

Over the years, Wilson and her longtime coach, Derek Thompson, settled on a counterintuitive guiding motto: Hard work should be easy. "Yes, it's challenging, it's hard," Wilson says, "but let's try to create an environment where it's easy to get it done."

Keeping a Natural Pulse

Wilson's pulsed approach to daily pacing feels renegade in a culture that prizes consistent, dogged progress. Yet the idea of aligning bursts of effort with natural rhythms isn't new; to some extent, it recalls older, more intuitive ways of structuring the day. Midday siestas have been part of Indigenous cultures for thousands of years, and in the Middle Ages, laborers took both midmorning and midafternoon breaks. In 1797, German physician Christoph Wilhelm Hufeland advocated for honoring what he called "natural chronology": working when energy levels were predictably highest and retreating when they ebbed.

But by the Industrial Revolution, traditional break rhythms started to fall by the wayside, eclipsed by strict work schedules that managed each worker's time down to the minute—all to benefit employers that profited handsomely from this setup. Yet many workers, aware that their alertness naturally rose and fell, found ways to resist the clock's tyranny. A 1951 *Time* magazine article described office workers' habit of dipping out for short coffee breaks, then slipping back in without being noticed. "No time clock daunts the coffee-breakers," the reporter wrote, "and no office manager's frown." (Ironically, this subversion likely worked to companies' benefit: Studies have since shown that when employees take breaks, they focus better on the next task at hand.)

But as US workplaces grew more regimented and specialized, the clock increasingly won the upper hand. Coffee breaks and leisurely lunches yielded to back-to-back meetings and desk-side takeout, a change spurred in part by the workday's changing architecture. As people shared their online calendars with colleagues and scheduled meetings with a button click, they found themselves more beholden to the tick of the minute hand.

With these shifts came the rise of the time-management movement, which promised that you could supercharge your productivity by charting your day in fifteen-minute, half-hour, or other timed increments. The idea has proved so enticing to Americans that time-management books like *The Time-Block Planner* by Cal Newport have consistently sold like hotcakes.

Many time-management experts do concede that people need to take breaks during the day. To address this need, however, they often recommend blocking or "chunking"—filling your day with digestible, timed work periods and fitting your timed rest breaks in between. One of the most popular chunking methods involves banging out "pomodoros": twenty-five-minute work periods capped by five-minute breaks, followed by another round of the same when your rest time is up.

But ultra-regimented time-management approaches, notes mental-skills trainer Colleen Hacker, tend to run counter to basic biology. Humans have natural energy peaks and valleys throughout the day, and shrewd pacing requires working with those natural rhythms, not against them. "The era of time management has passed," says Hacker, who has worked with members of the US Olympic soccer and hockey teams. "The term I use is 'energy management.'"

Riding Your Energy Peaks

Among the biggest misconceptions about virtuosos, no matter their chosen domain, is that they have a singular ability to stay on task no matter what. The truth, Hacker says, is that they are subject to the same energetic ups and downs as anyone else—and as a result, their capacity for meaningful effort varies throughout the day.

What people like Ajeé Wilson have mastered is a fine-tuned sense of when to bear down and when to back off, guided by knowledge of when their best windows of focus appear. For many people, one of these critical energetic peaks falls in mid- to late morning. Researchers who've mapped alertness, attention, and performance over twenty-four-hour spans have found that most people reach attention peaks a few hours after awakening. After lunch, you'll likely hit a notable lag, followed by another energetic peak in the afternoon or early evening.

Some researchers have zoomed in further, mapping so-called ultra-dian rhythms—patterns of alertness and fatigue that vary frequently throughout the day. Studies of these cycles show that many people focus best for about one or two hours at a time before their attention starts to drift. If you don't take at least a short break at the end of these focused stints, your efforts to stay on task are likely to falter.

Through trial and error, Wilson has discovered that she tends to have an energy surge in mid- to late morning, just as biorhythm studies might predict. Her daily workouts go best when she starts them around 10:00 a.m., once she feels fully awake.

A typical workout for Wilson consists of a series of mid-length runs. To make world-level teams, Derek Thompson explains, Wilson needs to maintain her endurance by stacking runs of various lengths—for instance, two 600-meter runs, followed by three 500s and four 400s. These runs are interspersed with short breaks so she can catch her breath and prepare for the next stint.

Having worked together for more than a decade, Wilson and Thompson trust each other implicitly. She relies on him to help her figure out the best training pace, and he, in turn, trusts her to stay the overall course.

That means Wilson gets a lot of say about how each training day plays out. If intense endurance training gets too painful or exhausting, she and

Thompson will confer and come up with a different plan for that day. The overall cadence of one training session might look quite different from the next, depending on her alertness, her body's response to initial run stints, and her inner reckoning about how much she can handle.

This flexible approach to daily pacing, informed by biological rhythms, pays off no matter the task at hand. For years, New York City real estate broker Nikki Beauchamp tried to conform to the nine-to-five work schedule so many of her colleagues had embraced. When Beauchamp felt depleted during the day, "I used to really try to push through," she says. "Somehow I convinced myself just to keep going, right into the wall." During these lulls, her progress would be so sluggish that her frustration would balloon—and that angst became its own kind of distraction.

Beauchamp started to reconsider her approach when she heard a presentation that addressed the natural ebbs and flows in human alertness. During the talk, she had a sudden realization: *Wow, that's why I sometimes need a twenty-minute break after working for an hour.*

After that insight, Beauchamp experimented with following her body's lead—launching straight into projects when she awakened in the morning with a great idea, or riding late-night bursts of energy, but also allowing herself to nap without guilt when she hit a wall. "I keep circling back to, 'I will work when it suits me the best,'" she says. "Why try to force myself into a pattern that's not natural?"

To get a better sense of my own natural patterns, I decide to try a similar tactic. For years, I've used the Pomodoro method to chart twenty-five-minute-long work blocks throughout the day, each one followed by a five-minute break. But since circadian-rhythm studies suggest I might be primed for more intense focus around midmorning, I decide to try settling in for longer writing stints—anywhere from forty-five minutes to an hour and a half, depending on how my focus holds up.

For the most part, the studies' findings hold true. When I start work around 9:30 or 10:00, I often feel immersed enough after the first half hour that I decide to continue without wedging in another short break. This decision doesn't feel like a feat of willpower; it feels more like going with the flow.

To map out your own pulsed approach to reaching any goal you've chosen, figure out where your high-energy windows typically fall during the day. While you might have some sense of whether you identify as a night owl or an early riser, labels like these don't matter as much as does your answer to a core question: When does focused progress feel more like moving with the current rather than swimming against it?

As you consider this question, think about what times of day you've typically been most creative or energetic, or when you find it easiest to shut out distractions. "For some people, it's first thing in the morning. A few people would tell you that it's late afternoon," Hacker says. "There's not *one* answer, but there's *an* answer that you really have to doggedly protect." If you have a creative vocation, honoring a peak window might mean disabling your internet connection during that time so you can focus on what needs to get done. If you're pursuing a goal unrelated to your day job, you might consider taking work shifts outside your high-focus window so you can use that window to pursue what you're most invested in.

While the timing of peak-focus windows varies from one person to the next, research suggests that taking advantage of such windows—no matter when they may fall—is integral to thriving. After reviewing more than thirty thousand Americans' daily routines, Wharton School marketing professor Marissa Sharif found that people who regularly had more than five hours of unscheduled free time every day were less happy than those who had a more moderate amount—from two to five hours. This tallies with endocrinologist Hans Selye's theory that taking on measured amounts of "eustress," or good stress, is actually healthy.

Too much slack time, as Wharton study coauthor Cassie Holmes explains, can drain the sense of purpose that drives flourishing. As you embark on sustaining stretches of focus, however, keep their length manageable—perhaps a single ultradian cycle of one to two hours. (Importantly, the focused time that anchors you doesn't have to be devoted to paid work, so long as it is spent on a meaningful task or pursuit.)

It's completely fine, and biologically appropriate, for the boundaries of your focus windows to be fuzzy. Ajeé Wilson doesn't worry much if she starts her workouts at 10:15 or 10:20 instead of ten o'clock sharp, and Nikki Beauchamp doesn't worry whether she starts work on a big project at 4:00 or 4:30 p.m.

Though some managers swear by time-block scheduling, priding themselves on never drifting from the plan, deliberate pacing calls for more open-endedness and give. Too-exact scheduling can backfire, not just because it's brittle and impractical but also because it creates an under-the-gun sense of time pressure that can interfere with meaningful progress. Faced with hard-and-fast time limits, people not only feel more stressed but fall back on rote thinking in the interest of efficiency, rather than taking the risk of innovation. In this way, boxing in a project can undermine some of the reasons for doing it in the first place.

Slotting in Micro-Breaks

Skilled pacers like Ajeé Wilson follow a responsive, pulsed approach even *during* their windows of peak effort. Wilson has grown adept, for instance, at sprinkling micro-breaks into her most focused work stints. As she finishes each set of workout runs, she approaches Derek Thompson for a quick chat, then checks out for a few minutes. On some breaks, she takes a few bites of a green apple and a swig of water. On others, she leans her body on the fence and stares off into the distance. These brief recovery moments, she says, allow her to "get it together, keep it together."

During most of Wilson's short breaks, she moves her body as little as possible—and new research supports that approach: The less related a micro-break activity is to what you do on the clock, the more restored you're likely to feel afterward. In a study of breaks lasting ten minutes or less, people who did work-related tasks during their breaks felt more depleted and had worse moods afterward, while those who did something unrelated to their job (catching up with a friend, exercising) felt better and more energetic hours later.

Nikki Beauchamp, too, has learned that to get a true mental reset during short breaks, she has to do something completely different from brainstorming or responding to emails. "I might grab my dog, go for a walk, go get a frozen yogurt," she says. Even getting up and walking around her apartment works better than trying to destress at her desk.

Just as important as how you decide to spend your micro-breaks is how much control you feel over those decisions. A study at Finland's Tampere University found that the more say people have about how they spend their short breaks, the more recovered they report feeling when they return to work.

Maintaining control over her training rhythm, on a micro and macro basis, helps keep Wilson thriving in her sport. What's key, she says, is "tweaking and trying to find the right balance." To maintain this balance, Thompson tells Wilson to decide what kind of downtime she needs during any given workout. "He lets me just follow my body, find my rhythm, and find my pace."

Bookending Effort with Equal Recovery

Though Wilson's daily workouts may be intense, they're also surprisingly brief. Her main workout lasts only about two hours, and near the end of it, she's depleted enough that she knows she'll risk injury and mental exhaustion if she continues. Her schedule smashes the stereotype of the

Olympic athlete toiling from sunup to sundown, but she's hardly alone in tackling her day's most important work in one or two intense pulses. In a Norwegian study of cross-country skiers and other endurance athletes, all of whom had won at least one world or Olympic gold medal, athletes trained an average of eight hundred hours a year, which works out to just over two hours a day.

These energy and focus limits also apply outside the athletic realm. After two to four hours of creatively demanding work each day, most people feel too drained to make much additional progress, and in a survey of nearly two thousand office workers, most respondents reported doing less than three hours of productive work each day, on average. (Much of their clocked-in time was actually spent catching up with coworkers, checking social media, making coffee, or reading the news.)

Once your focused work is done, it's crucial to take a rest period commensurate with the effort you've put forth. "What do you do after your workout is done for the day?" I ask Ajeé Wilson, expecting her to reel off hobbies or favorite nighttime haunts. She laughs. "Sleep!" Once she gets home from her daily workout and lunch, she says, she often collapses on her bed and stays out cold for hours. Essentially, it's a traditional siesta, extended to match the intensity of her morning workout.

Like Wilson, Beauchamp has learned to embrace what Italians call *il dolce far niente*—the sweetness of doing nothing. When she's had a chaotic week, she often devotes her whole Saturday to rest. "I don't even leave my apartment," she says. "I just need an entire day when I sit on the couch. I nap on and off all day, because that's what my body wants."

No matter the task at hand, recovery periods that match the effort you've exerted help keep apathy and burnout at bay. What often shocks people outside the athletic world, Colleen Hacker says, is just how many hours pros spend at rest, especially in the days before and after a high-stakes event. In her view, that's exactly as it should be, on the competitive field and off. Many athletes have seen the rewards of cutting back their training right before a competition—a tactic known as tapering, which reliably improves performance the day of the event.

To be sure, sensible pacing plans often include intense stretches of effort. There are times when you'll need to pull extra shifts, train extra hours, or spend a weekend making a presentation before a conference crowd. But to maintain a measured overall pace, you might need to take several days to decompress after an unusually stressful week or after a major presentation or event.

If this level of decompression seems out of reach, given your schedule's constraints, you can still use the time windows you do have for maximum recovery benefits. On your next weekend or day off after a major push, choose activities that feel most restful to you—long naps, yoga sessions, even judicious "bed rotting"—rather than all-day drives or hikes. You can also facilitate decompression with some advance planning, slotting in vacation days right after what you know will be your most intense weeks of the year.

Athletes in various disciplines use an approach called "periodization" to set this kind of staggered pace, deliberately following intense-training days with low-intensity days to avoid injury and exhaustion. This approach evolved in part out of findings that maximum performance can be maintained only for brief stretches of time. Other research shows that when employees in a wide range of fields set a flexible rhythm of effort and rest, they feel less stressed and more satisfied on the job.

Without the release valve of rest that is proportional to exerted effort, a vicious cycle can take hold. Not only will skimping on recovery time make it harder to perform the next day, but the extra effort you'll have to muster to do so will leave you feeling even more depleted—and at that point, taking a longer stretch of time off may be the only way to replenish your energy stores.

Navigating Daily Stalls and Crises

While circadian experts often refer to the body's "inner clocks," natural energy cycles aren't as predictable as clockwork; a multitude of factors affect them from one day to the next. If you hardly slept the night before, your focus window the following morning may not last as long as it normally would, and if you're grappling with a big move or a family crisis, your usual daily rhythm might go completely out the window.

Fluctuations like these can be especially challenging if you're ill or disabled, since your baseline energy levels may be lower to begin with. To navigate their energetic peaks and valleys, people with conditions like chronic fatigue, lupus, or multiple sclerosis often practice "activity pacing," either on their own or assisted by doctors.

Activity pacers begin by figuring out what exertion levels typically cause them to tire (say, twenty minutes of hard exercise or two Zoom meetings in a row), and they plan their days to include breaks once they've reached these exertion benchmarks. Those break periods, dubbed "pre-emptive rest," are designed to stave off the physical or mental crashes that come with pushing too hard for too long. Practitioners also become skilled at ongoing, reflective assessment, asking themselves how much energy they have left, then scaling their plans up or down accordingly.

Activity pacing is one version of what exercise scientists call "teleoanticipation"—gauging the energy you have left and controlling its release so you don't run out before reaching a given finish line (the end of a race, a day or a project). The more you practice this kind of anticipatory pacing, the better you get at it and the more intuitive it becomes.

The responsive energy assessments that activity pacers do daily can benefit almost anyone who faces unexpected daily disruptions, or who finds themself facing physical or mental overwhelm.

Through the years, I've found that I tend to get stalled out during stressful weeks when I'm frantic about just how much I need to get done.

At those moments, I explain to Amy Baltzell, I feel like I'm mentally hyperventilating, and just getting through the day feels like a grueling slog.

To pace yourself through daily stalled-out moments, Baltzell advises getting into a calmer state before you make any decisions. You can do this by conducting a sort of detached assessment—not fleeing what's in front of you, but naming it objectively, without exaggeration: *I have two reports due tomorrow, and I need to do several hours of work on each. I slept for three hours last night.*

So many of us make the mistake of steamrolling our own physical and mental limits because we don't let ourselves acknowledge when we've hit them. Pausing to take an objective read on what's going on helps you to accept your limits when they arise, and to choose the best response for the situation at hand—one that helps conserve your remaining energy.

With a calmer, more realistic outlook, it's easier to navigate the broad middle of the pacing spectrum, as runners and activity pacers do on a regular basis. Instead of just powering through your to-do list no matter what, or swiftly deciding you're so overburdened you need to take the day off, you can ask yourself what you actually need at this moment—which might end up being a half-hour jog, a strategy session with a colleague, or a fifteen-minute vent to a friend. After that, you can sketch out the rest of your day, or your week, based on how energetic you're feeling. "It's not all or nothing," Baltzell says. "It's 'What's the wise choice here?'"

Embracing Rigid Flexibility

As Ajeé Wilson has found, this responsive approach to daily challenges meshes well with routines that are as frictionless as possible. Wilson's rigid flexibility principle rests on three pillars: Tackle your most intense work when it feels least arduous, based on your natural energy cycles. After sustained effort, take a long-enough rest to meaningfully replenish your body and mind—even if that means defying hard-charging cultural expectations. Finally, make a practice of noticing when you've hit a wall and need to shift course, whether you saw that wall coming or not. Rigid flexibility creates a healthy tension between commitment and give that spurs ongoing flourishing.

Taking a cue from this approach, more employers are beginning to adopt scheduling practices conducive to flexible, pulsed rhythms of effort and rest. Some elastic shift arrangements require employees to report for a set period of a few hours, but allow them to choose their own arrival, departure, and break times on either side of that window. It's a structure that lets employees crank out more high-level work when it feels easiest and fade out when their focus naturally drifts.

As Ajeé Wilson plans for a future after athletics, she'll continue to embrace this flexible approach. "The path that I've taken so far has been kind of nontraditional. We've made it our own as we've gone," Wilson says. That gives her confidence that no matter what she does next, she'll be able to maintain the work habits she's perfected—going all out when her energy crests, then retreating to assess what she needs before the next push, a strategy she knows will serve her in almost any domain.

Chapter 5

The Art of Modulation

When **Joe Arpaia** was in medical school, he spent a harrowing night in the emergency room—one that would bend the arc of his career.

Arpaia was part of the trauma team that night, assigned to handle any urgent case that came in. As the clock inched toward midnight, the ER doors swung open, and staff wheeled in a car-accident victim with profuse internal bleeding from the abdomen. Members of the trauma team rushed to the man's bedside, their mandate clear: open up the abdomen and figure out exactly where the bleeding was coming from. "I'm holding suction and trying to clear the field," Arpaia remembers, "keep the blood from obscuring the doctor's vision."

The steady red freshet in the abdomen meant the critical wound was likely nearby: an injury to the man's aorta, maybe, or the liver. But no matter how hard the team members looked, they couldn't find a tell-tale breach. "Everything was intact," Arpaia says. "And he's leaving the planet."

The trauma team's leader that night was Dr. Miller, one of the ER's most experienced surgeons. As blood kept pooling in the wound cavity, Miller did something unexpected: He stopped, stood back, and took a sustained deep breath. "I remember just watching him [do] a long exhale, his shoulders settle and pause," Arpaia says. That pause, taking no more than a few seconds, seemed to crystallize something for Miller. He signaled Arpaia to move his suction tube higher. "He tells me, 'Up here, by the diaphragm.'"

When Arpaia repositioned the tube and sucked the blood away, he saw it: a ragged, inch-long tear with fresh blood bubbling through it. The accident had torn a hole through the diaphragm. As the team scrutinized that tear, they quickly found the critical wound, which was in the right chamber of the patient's heart. Dr. Miller's intuitive hunch, which allowed the trauma team to mend the tear swiftly, saved the man's life.

Through the years, Arpaia has found himself thinking about that chaotic night. He remembers the fizz of panic as the team worked to find where the blood was coming from, the rising sense that their efforts were futile. As a mid-career psychiatrist in the 1990s, Arpaia began treating dozens of clients marinating in that kind of panic, or the extended-release version of it. Their nervous systems seemed overclocked—their heart rates raced, and their shoulders perpetually tensed up. Many grappled with demanding lives and careers. In their perpetually stressed state, they struggled to make thoughtful decisions about their lives, and the fallout of their worst missteps sometimes followed them for years, scuttling their efforts to find stability.

As Arpaia considered how best to help his clients, he thought about how his ER mentor had responded when the wounded patient was leaving the planet. How he'd disengaged to take a long, deep breath—and how after that deliberate disengagement, he'd summoned the solution that had seemed so elusive before.

Ultimately, that example helped inspire an approach Arpaia began using with his overstressed clients, training them to practice what he called "unease modulation," or modulation, for short. His rationale was simple: Once they learned how to ease themselves reliably into less frantic states, they could summon clearer thinking in tense moments and make decisions that would better serve them in the long run.

As an everyday pacing strategy, modulation brims with untapped potential. It can quell your fight-or-flight response faster than anxiety medication. It offers renewal and a chance to slow down during stressful moments, enough to make navigating difficult days seem manageable. If you're bad at meditating, it's a viably mindful alternative. And in creating physical calm, it ushers in states of mind that allow you to make better decisions in the moment—the kinds of decisions that conserve your energy, helping you pace yourself over the long term. It can even instill the kind of composure that gives rise to life-saving insights like Dr. Miller's. Yet modulation also requires a kind of resolute self-distancing: the capacity, and the willingness, to step back from what's happening to you at the precise moment it's hardest to pull yourself away.

Containing the Chaos

Long before Joe Arpaia became a doctor, he was fascinated with chaos theory. As an undergrad at Caltech, he'd studied complex chemical systems with many interacting components. What stuck with him was that when a single component went awry, it disrupted the balance of the entire system.

That insight surfaced again later in his career, when Arpaia was inundated with psychiatric clients who seemed perpetually unable to destress. Many of his colleagues scheduled such patients for fifteen- or twenty-minute sessions, prescribing them medication, and sending them on their way. In the 1990s, "psychiatry was very biologic," Arpaia says. "Serotonin, dopamine, and norepinephrine were the answer to everything." Yet antidepressants, though useful, were not working as well as advertised for many of his patients. Arpaia dove into longer talk therapy sessions with them to figure out why they still felt so revved up all the time. "I'd see people for forty-five, fifty minutes. I just kept trying to understand and listen."

In those sessions, Arpaia began to notice how closely his clients' symptoms tracked what was happening in their lives. If stress flared for very long—whether due to work problems, family obligations, or relationship issues—their depressed moods, headaches, and anger outbursts flared as well. When they were in what he came to call an "activated state," they often made poor choices that undermined their lives and relationships, kicking off yet another round of stress.

That downward spiral got Arpaia thinking about how to teach clients to blunt stress's physical effects before they interfered with decision-making. The approach he chose drew on biofeedback research that showed people could be taught to regulate physical responses once thought beyond their control.

Most people breathe unconsciously at a speed of more than a dozen breaths per minute, a pace that bears little relationship to how calm or stressed they're feeling. But when they take slower breaths—between four and eight per minute, depending on the person—their heart rate starts to speed up more dramatically as they breathe in, and then slow down more dramatically as they breathe out. This breathing speed is known as the "resonant frequency."

The more someone's heart rate changes from in-breath to out-breath, the higher their heart rate variability score, a marker linked to physical resilience and well-being. Breathing at resonant frequency speeds also stimulates the vagus nerve, which transmits signals to the brain that tamp down blood pressure and induce calm. As Arpaia showed his clients how to do resonant frequency breathing exercises, he noticed their outlook gradually growing more tempered, their reactions to curveballs less pronounced.

People like Wade Warren, a retired vet and probation officer who'd been practicing modulation techniques for years, confirmed Arpaia's sense of the techniques' power. Warren first learned about paced breathing before a military deployment to Iraq. Not only did the practice restore his composure when he was under fire but learning the technique before his deployment also helped him face the months and years afterward, as he processed what he'd been through on the battlefield.

"A lot of the work that I did was preventative," Warren says, something his doctors confirmed during post-deployment care. If he hadn't been using modulation techniques, he says, "I'd have a pretty serious case of PTSD."

The Basics of Modulation

As someone who knows what it feels like to operate in a panicked haze—to muscle through each day with jaw clenched and shoulders hunched to my ears—I'm curious to see what kind of difference Arpaia's approach can make for me.

Once Arpaia sits me down and clips a monitor on my finger, my heart rate tracing starts scrolling across a laptop screen, a frenetic series of spikes and valleys. "Here you can see you activate fairly strongly," Arpaia says, pointing to the tracing, which jumps erratically when I open my mouth to speak. On some level, I think I've always known this about myself. When a fire alarm goes off, I'm the one who jumps the highest, and when I speak in front of groups, my heart rate soars into the stratosphere.

Next, Arpaia walks me through the basics of unease-modulation practice. He starts by playing a series of audio recordings with the words "calm" and "relax" overlaid on a track of ocean waves. The words serve as a guide: "Calm" cues me to breathe in and "relax" to breathe out. This guided breathing, Arpaia says, will help him identify my resonant frequency breathing pace, which will be much slower than the unconscious breathing most people do. "Normal respiration rates are twelve to fifteen breaths per minute. The average resonant frequency is around six breaths per minute. And almost all adults are between, I would say, four and eight."

Arpaia cues up the first audio track. "The most important thing is, does the rate feel comfortable?" he says. "If it feels uncomfortable, let me know." Once he presses Play, I close my eyes and start breathing, matching my in- and out-breaths to "calm" and "relax." But after a few deep breaths, I start to feel dizzy, and I tell him the pace feels too fast.

"That's exactly what I was picking up," Arpaia says. "I'm going to slow it down." He clicks on another audio file, and I resume the exercise, breathing in on "calm" and out on "relax." This time, my breathing speed feels effortless, and I continue to breathe with the guided track.

After a few minutes, Arpaia pauses the audio and scrolls back through my recorded heart rate tracings. "Here's where you started doing the breathing." He points to a spot where my characteristic spikes soften into gentle, shallow curves—the kind of characteristic waves I've seen in research papers, showing a rise in heart rate variability. "Your heart rate changed pattern within three seconds," Arpaia says. "If I had an IV in your arm, and I pushed a sedative, it would take a good twenty-some seconds to take effect. This is faster than an IV medication. It's almost instantaneous."

Arpaia then shows me another modulation exercise to use when I'm especially tense, which he calls the "long exhale" or "reset breath." "You take a breath in and you blow out through pursed lips," he says. I gulp air and focus on letting it out slowly, as if through a straw. When I open my eyes, my lungs emptied, I see a pronounced dip in my tracing on the laptop screen. "Your heart rate dropped twenty beats a minute," Arpaia says.

I'm genuinely surprised at how quickly the exercises have eased me into physical calm. Internally, it feels as if a jar lid has been loosened, letting air into a stagnant space. It's too soon to tell, of course, but I wonder if this refreshed state might give rise to thoughts and ideas that wouldn't have occurred to me a few minutes before.

One way to figure out your own resonant-breathing frequency is to use an app like Elite HRV or BreathTuner. Apps like these, when used with a wearable heart rate tracker, guide you through a series of breathing exercises at different speeds, allowing you to select the one that feels most comfortable. In some apps, you can observe in real time the effects of a given breathing frequency on your HRV.

You can also try playing audio tracks—available on YouTube and elsewhere—that guide you in breathing between four and eight breaths per minute, depending on the track. The pace that feels most comfortable to you is likely to be close to your resonant frequency, whether you confirm it with an app or not.

In the beginning, commit to breathing at your resonant pace for several minutes straight, so it will start to feel more natural. At a time you choose, or when you feel stressed, cue up the audio track or launch your HRV app. Assess how you feel at the end of your initial breathing stint, and if you still feel unsettled, continue breathing at the same pace for another few minutes.

After a week or so of practicing with apps or audio tracks, Arpaia says, many people no longer need these aids to fall into their resonant-breathing rhythm. "I say, 'Breathe comfortably,' and they'll be really, really close to that frequency. Their body learns it very quickly."

Once this breathing rhythm becomes more intuitive, you can start to do resonant breathing just when your stress levels spike, or when the pace of your life ramps up—when you're preparing to launch into an overnight shift or give a presentation for a large audience. At especially tense moments, during emergencies or other events that throw you off axis, you can deploy the long exhale to make your stress response plummet quickly.

As resonant breathing instills physical calm, it also restores the mental equilibrium that will allow you to choose the best possible course of action, which may mean making a significant pace or mentality shift to accommodate whatever you're facing. Modulation helps usher in what researchers call metacognition, which is the ability to evaluate your own thinking—an ability that allows for fluid pace changes and can foster better mental health.

Now that he's left the military, Wade Warren often calls on his modulation skills in situations like high-stakes meetings or difficult conversations. Once, when Warren was leaving a job, a work colleague tried needling him during his exit interview, suggesting that he'd rigged the competition for a national award he'd won.

Though Warren felt an impulse to fire back in kind—something he might have done when he was younger—taking focused breaths helped him tamp down his aggression and remember why he was there in the first place: to wrap up this phase of his career and move on. So, instead of escalating the exchange, Warren remembers, "I just said, 'You probably don't want to try this with anybody else,'" and he got out of the situation as soon as he could. Not only did this muted response keep Warren feeling steady in the moment, it prevented him from engaging in a draining (and pointless) pissing contest. Warren has led modulation trainings for other probation officers, hoping the practice can help them conserve their energy and make shrewd decisions under pressure.

Joe Arpaia, too, has put the exercises at the center of a self-calming routine he's maintained for years. At the end of a long workday, before he rejoins his family, "I do a bit of recovery breathing in the car for a couple of minutes and then come in the door," he says. "What this technique does is help you shift into your recharge state. It's almost like regaining your balance."

Arpaia's split-second recharge tactics have paid dividends. Not only do they replenish his inner reserves, they keep him from expending his energy in futile or destructive ways. One afternoon, when his teenage daughter got home from school, she marched straight up to her room and shut the door, hard. Right away, Arpaia was on edge. He was exhausted himself, and his heart rate accelerated as his inner monologue turned indignant. "There was this instant activation—'You know, that's not right. She's ignoring me. That's disrespectful and blah, blah, blah.'"

Rather than marching up to his daughter's room and demanding to know why she'd acted that way, Arpaia did a long, exhaling reset breath. Afterward, a new possibility appeared to him, like an outline in a dark-room bath. "I didn't really hear the door slam," he says. "It was just me getting activated and then mistakenly perceiving the door slammed."

The facts, he realized, were these: His daughter had come home, silently headed to her room, and closed the door. He went up and calmly asked her what was going on, and she replied that she'd just had a long day. When he asked her if she wanted some tea, she said yes. He prepared the tea and mulled over the potential blowup he'd been able to deflect—an outcome that, given the stakes, felt miraculous.

If he'd gone up to his daughter's room on a high horse, he reflected, it might have taken months to fix things. A blowup would have created immeasurably more stress for them both, and it would have meant he'd need to repair an important relationship on top of everything else on his plate. To pull off that repair, he'd have had to exhaust his own emotional reserves. But by keeping on an even keel, moment by moment, he'd maintained a steadier, more measured pace—and fostered a trusting bond he hoped would last through his daughter's growing-up years and beyond.

Modulating Your Biology

While research on resonant breathing's effects is still underway, initial studies underscore its power to instill and maintain calm. In one Brigham Young University study, researchers split ninety-five participants into three groups. One group breathed at their resonant frequency for fifteen minutes, the second group breathed slightly faster than their resonant frequency, and the third did not control their breathing at all. Following this fifteen-minute block, all the participants took a challenging mental math test.

Throughout, the experimenters assessed the participants' heart rate variability, blood pressure, and mood. While all the groups had similar vital stats at the outset, members of the resonant frequency group scored higher on a mood scale after the fifteen-minute guided exercise. Their blood pressure was also less reactive during the mental math test, which hinted they were experiencing less physical stress, even though they were tackling a difficult task.

The exercise's calming effects also persist throughout the day with regular practice. In a study that compared people who did twenty straight minutes of daily resonant frequency breathing to people in a control group, the first group had more heart rate variability improvement after four weeks, a sign that their bodies were becoming more relaxed overall.

Such physical changes can usher in major changes in real-world performance and well-being. Arpaia and his University of Toronto colleague Judith Andersen demonstrated this when they gave hundreds of police officers a weeks-long course in modulation skills. In addition to paced breathing, the officers learned a long-exhale reset-breath technique like the one Arpaia showed me. After the training, the officers performed better at work across the board, and they were also more apt to recover quickly from stressful events.

Departments around the country have approached Arpaia and Andersen for training, eager to help officers resolve inner states that can trigger instant catastrophe. On the force, the difference between a calm nervous system and an overactive one can mean approaching a suspect peacefully rather than killing them in an errant burst of gunfire.

Putting Modulation to the Test

For a policeman or surgeon, a split-second decision can alter the course of a career—or a life. But for those of us who don't navigate life-or-death scenarios, the effect of individual small decisions is more subtle, accreting gradually over time.

To gauge how Joe Arpaia's practices affect my own outlook and pace-setting in the longer term, I commit to a modulation trial lasting at least two weeks, at which point I'll decide whether to extend the trial. The day I start, things are looking rough. A close friend has just lost her mother, days after another friend's toddler died in a tragic accident. On top of that, bombings and civilian attacks are ramping up in the Middle East, and a firestorm of recriminations is rising around the world, along with the death toll. I've started waking up with heart-pounding bursts of anxiety that seem like the worst kind of omen.

I begin with a five-minute stint of resonance breathing each day, with plans to add more breathing time if my stress rebounds during the day. Arpaia has clocked my resonant frequency rate at about 5.2 breaths per minute, so I cue up a YouTube video that narrates guided in- and out-breaths at that speed as a low-pitched synth plays in the background.

After my first five-minute block on day one, I feel more relaxed, just as I did at the end of my session with Arpaia. Though the rubber band–ball at the base of my stomach hasn't gone away, it feels as if it's loosened. The world still seems to be heading to hell in a handbasket, but my relationship to that surrounding hell has shifted by a few degrees.

For the remainder of the week, I cue up the YouTube video each day to help me pace my breaths for five minutes at a stretch. Just as Arpaia predicted, my resonant-breathing speed seems to imprint on me, becoming more intuitive with each passing day.

Moving into the second week, as I prepare for work calls or wait in the car at long lights, I find myself shifting spontaneously into my breathing rhythm without cues from the video, sometimes without consciously intending to do so. Once in a while, I even find myself craving that particular breathing pace. The practice is starting to feel like a relief, a release of pressure.

As my trial morphs into a daily, ingrained practice, I grow more adept at using Arpaia's method to quell the mental firestorms. When a reported story of mine goes through an intense fact-checking process, with endless questions peppering my inbox, I start to worry I've made huge mistakes that will soon be exposed. I check my email every few minutes, half expecting a message the story is riddled with errors and will have to be scrapped. Objectively, I know this isn't likely, but my sympathetic nervous system is drowning out the logical thoughts. The large vessels in my neck pound, and my body hunches forward, as if curling itself around something fragile.

Recognizing a descending anxiety spiral, I launch into my unease-modulation routine. My breathing naturally settles into a rhythm similar to the resonant pace I've been training myself to keep.

Over the years, I've gotten used to my heart rate revving up within seconds when a catastrophic thought—*My editor will know how badly I screwed up*—consumes me. But as I continue to breathe and my heart rate ratchets down, the tone of the thoughts looping in the background shifts, not dramatically, but perceptibly.

The change isn't instantaneous, like a switch clicking off. There is a spin-down period before the aggrieved thoughts evaporate and other, more measured ones wend their way in. *If I made a mistake, we'll get to fix it. Better now than after publication.* If I'd remained frantic, it would be easier to make rash, undermining moves: firing off an aggrieved email to my editor, castigating myself harshly enough to trigger a depressive episode.

I come to recognize in the following weeks that modulation instills this kind of detachment better than my past meditation efforts have. Meditation tends to trip me up because it takes all my concentration, and when my attention wanders—say, to a thought about tonight's dinner or next week's deadlines—I struggle to get it back.

Resonant breathing doesn't require this level of undivided attention. You can keep your resonant-breathing pace on semi-autopilot while scanning the news or scrolling through email. And once the practice becomes effortless, you can deploy it whenever you feel like you're spinning into an anxious state, rather than every day.

As you begin to use modulation, reflect on any changes you notice: whether your internal monologue changes during tense moments, and whether that shift subtly influences the choices you make. Getting into a calmer physical state makes it easier to pace yourself through the day, on an hour-by-hour basis, to ask yourself, *What's the wise choice here?* As modulation turns into an established habit, this calmer state starts to become your new default—the baseline from which everything else proceeds.

How Modulation Alters Your Decision Tree

The cardinal question surrounding any practice that calls for behavioral change is this: Can the routine last, not for a few days but for years on end—long enough that it becomes part of your mind's architecture, replicating itself by default?

Though I haven't practiced modulation nearly as long as Joe Arpaia or Wade Warren, I do know that over the course of more than a year, I've come to depend on the practice as a way of pacing myself through daily stresses, partly because it flows in and around and through everything else that's going on. While it's tough to multitask when you're meditating, you can do Arpaia's breathing practice while you're chopping vegetables, reading, or walking to work.

Amid a smorgasbord of pacing strategies, modulation also stands out for the fine-grained control it gives you over your physical state. By practicing resonant breathing for different lengths of time, you can move into the precise state of calm or alertness the moment calls for. If you're about to give a presentation, you'll want to be centered yet alert, whereas if you're winding down at the end of the day, you can progress all the way to complete calm. Anxiety medication is like a blunt hammer by comparison, since it may take a half hour to kick in and often overshoots the mark.

When I hit a wall during the day, growing anxious or overwhelmed, I used to try to reason myself out of it, only to watch my wheel-spinning mind deflect those attempts at reason, over and over. I now believe, as Arpaia does, that some physical states are incompatible with clear decision-making, and that they must be resolved before you can mull over what's actually happening, make a choice, and go on with your day.

Over time, modulation also clears the way for decisions shaped less by your fight-or-flight response and more by your own unclouded sense of what will help you thrive in the long run. Each modulation-guided choice—Arpaia's decision not to yell at his daughter, Warren's decision to step away from his workplace aggressor—can alter your entire decision tree. You can observe the tree's branching as you continue to practice modulation. In the aftermath of a tense or stressful moment, what options has modulation opened up for you that might not otherwise have existed? What future possibilities might extend from this fresh set of options?

When I do my modulation practice, in the brief moments between kid pickups and work calls and email blasts, I call up the image of Arpaia's surgical mentor: how Dr. Miller squared his shoulders, let out a breath, and signaled that the bleeding source was somewhere no one else had thought to look. How that insight allowed him to repair a near-fatal wound, changing the trajectory of his patient's life as well as his own.

I doubt any decision I make will ever have stakes as high. Yet there are chances each day for the smaller-scale renewal that stems from physical calm—and hones the compassionate focus that promotes long-term flourishing. The incremental self-repair of modulation helps fuel daily attempts at contribution, from split-second assists to bridge-building conversations, and each of these attempts builds momentum for future ones. Like Dr. Miller, we usually know on some level how to handle a situation that's veering out of control, threatening to eclipse everything else. It's a matter of creating the right conditions to access that knowledge when it's most needed.

Chapter 6

Digital Triage

As the year 2023 drew to a close, Noelle Frost realized she was spending more time on Instagram and Facebook than she'd ever intended. Some of that time was necessary: As a blogger and travel expert, part of her job was to post and interact with fans, and she carved out regular time to do just that.

The problems emerged when Frost was at loose ends, looking to relieve boredom. A passing thought—*Let me check Facebook, because I have a few minutes at my computer*—could put her on the glide path to hours of online scrolling. Afterward, she'd be left with a confused swirl of emotions. Some of what popped up in her feeds was intriguing or moving, but some posts upset her or reminded her what she was missing out on (mansion life, jaunts to exotic locales). Other posts were as hollow as soap bubbles. Spending so much time on social media and coming away with so little was getting more and more frustrating. "It's good if you want to kill time," she says, "but not if you want to get things done."

The anthropologist Natasha Dow Schüll, who's spent years studying slot gamblers, describes a repeating cycle of engagement she calls the "ludic loop." Each time people push a button and watch the machine spin out a line of cherries, the research shows, their brains flood with dopamine—the same "feel good" chemical that would slosh in if they'd just downed a shot of liquor or won the lottery. Over time, gamblers come to associate each slot pull with this burst of excitement, whether or not they win anything. That prompts them to feed the machine over and over, seemingly oblivious to anything outside the casino's walls.

But the ludic loop, however entrancing, has always been empty. After long stretches of machine play, gamblers rise from their seats groggy and disoriented, unsure where the past few hours of their lives have gone.

Like Schüll's slot pullers, many of us struggle to disengage from the online world as our momentary choices override our conscious intentions. The opportunity costs of such addictive engagement are vast. While a well-paced life includes alternate stretches of effort and recovery, the ludic loop creates a frenzied stasis that allows for neither full engagement nor complete withdrawal.

"We gorge on social media," says author and Slow Movement pioneer Carl Honoré. "We're just built to stuff ourselves when there's plenty. That locks us into an endless loop of trying to consume more and more." Every hour spent in the loop, meanwhile, is an hour that depletes energy and focus, stalling progress toward long-term flourishing.

But while consuming low-hanging digital fruit can scuttle your pacing plans, more deliberate online engagement can further them. When you head online with a clearer idea of what you're up to, the digital realm starts to look less like a blinking, beckoning, time-sucking arcade and more like a launch point for principled action.

In a world where online engagement is both necessary and corrosive, the best digital pacing strategies are less about shutting out the chaos entirely and more about charting a well-defined path through it—a path that furthers your own goals, not those of app creators eager to keep you scrolling. Whether you're online or off, abstaining from time-sucking habits often fails as a stand-alone measure. To make lasting pace shifts, it's better to replace those habits with others that actively help you to thrive.

Lost in the Ludic Loop

To draw and hold more eyeballs, software designers have figured out how to activate ludic-loop response patterns almost every time users pull out their devices. Social media feeds serve up a smorgasbord of content that triggers your brain's reward response, says Duke University researcher Jordan Etkin, because the apps are designed to feed you posts similar to those you've liked before. And the apps' notification pings evoke a Pavlovian response, sending you to your phone in search of the dopamine rush that arrives with a like, comment, or reply.

When participants in Temple University studies received likes on an app similar to Instagram, they showed more activity in brain areas that process rewarding stimuli, including the nucleus accumbens. (For context, the nucleus accumbens also activates when gamblers view pictures of slot machines.)

Each pleasure spike spurs you to seek another as you foresee how good you're going to feel as a result. After researchers trained monkeys to use a button that opened the door to a tasty snack, their dopamine-control neurons started to activate while they were anticipating their coming reward, before they actually received the snack itself.

But it's not just bursts of reward that keep you in a virtual trance; it's also spasms of hostility and righteousness. Programmers deliberately evoke users' anger by serving up controversial content (news of a political scandal, say), which keeps people commenting and refreshing. "The algorithms are really focused on negative topics, because that leads to more engagement," says psychiatrist Mona Amini. "Even if people aren't liking the photo or video or reel, they are commenting on it, they're sending it to others, saving it."

Whatever the initial trigger, once you get stuck in the ludic loop, your natural impulse to get up, take a walk, or grab a snack fades into the background, overridden by the stronger impulse to keep checking your feeds. "I found myself looking at my phone hundreds of times per day," the novelist John Green has written. "I was constantly checking—refreshing and refreshing, as if something truly fresh were just over the horizon." And the more often you refresh, the more that response pattern etches itself into your brain, making it ever more difficult to erase.

Time hurled down the Facebook or Twitter rabbit hole is time unavailable for the contemplation that's integral to sustainable pacing—the kind of reflection that feeds purpose and contribution. Before the social media universe hit its stride, I plowed through multiple books a week, many of which changed my perspective and helped make my work better. But as my Twitter and Instagram time grew, so did my stacks of unread books, and my motivation to dive into them plummeted.

Algorithms also sap the capacities we need to thrive in an increasingly complex world. Society's continued functioning, as well as the planet's, depends on our collective ability to take the long view—to anticipate worst-case scenarios and work steadily to avoid them.

But the online universe, like a windowless casino room, blots out this future-mindedness. University of California, San Francisco and Stanford University researchers have found that people who are juggling more media feeds at once have poorer long-term memory and perform worse on tasks that require them to pay sustained attention. Amid a smorgasbord of content churn, we prize the immediate, the near term, over what must be carefully thought out, planned for, agonized over. Flourishing requires depth and breadth of thought; online-engagement ploys, often devoid of connection to real life, tend to bob us to the surface and keep us there.

Digital spaces that teem with purposeless activity also sap our zest for life in the long run. Heavy digital-media users in one San Diego State University study were more than twice as likely as lighter users to say they were unhappy, and they were also twice as likely to report suicidal thoughts.

Having grasped this calculus, growing numbers of people—some of them well-known influencers—have decided to remove themselves from the online fray. Struggling with a perpetual need to consume more content and an inability to focus, author John Green opted to leave social media behind for a year. Actor Taron Egerton did the same, citing a lack of balance that had grown crippling. "It's hard to break away from a cycle that I've grown to find a bit addictive," he explained in an Instagram post. "I actually feel like my ability to sit and be present, read books, watch movies, and even seek out the company of people I love is eroding as a result."

Following Green and Egerton's lead, Noelle Frost told her blog readers that she'd be taking a monthlong social media break, which she hoped would give her time and space to revamp her online habits. "Going into the new year, I was thinking, *I have a lot of other things that I want to prioritize, and I don't necessarily want to be looking at social media all the time.*" She also relished the thought of breaking free from platforms she'd come to see as controlling. "It was just like a challenge. Can I do it? Will I be okay?"

The Limits of Time Limits

Bailing out of social media entirely might seem tempting if you're mired in digital overwhelm. But it's also akin to a nuclear option, one most of us hesitate to consider. A more popular pacing approach involves setting time limits on specific apps. Typically, these are "suggested limits," whereby you receive an alert once you've been on an app for a certain length of time (say, thirty minutes or an hour). The idea is that when you grow more aware of how much time you've spent on the app, you'll be more motivated to disengage.

Yet this approach doesn't work as well as many people expect, and scientists have figured out some of the reasons why. Etkin and her colleagues at Duke studied digital limit setting in an experiment where they let people decide how much of a five-minute time block they'd spend playing a game called Bubble Shooter. When players were alerted that they'd get a time-limit reminder after playing the game for three minutes, they actually spent *more* time on Bubble Shooter than players with no set reminder at all.

While this result might seem surprising, it jibes with other psychology findings. Left to their own devices with something enticing—whether a plate of cookies or an addictive app—most people start to feel slightly more uncomfortable with every cookie they scarf down or round of play they log, Etkin says. When that mounting discomfort outweighs the enjoyment they're getting, they walk away.

People who set online time limits, on the other hand, don't tend to feel much discomfort before their pre-set time is up. Pre-set limits serve as "psychological permission to spend any amount of time below the limit on that activity," Etkin says. "It's like you've given yourself a free pass." That means that if you allot yourself, say, a half hour or forty-five minutes on Instagram, you may spend nearly all that time on the platform—even if you would have left earlier without having set any limits.

Just as Etkin would predict, my own attempts at online limit setting have backfired spectacularly. A few months ago, I set precise time limits on my computer with the help of built-in software: thirty minutes for one social media site, fifteen minutes for another. When my limit was up, a pop-up window let me know I'd reached that limit. Not only did I often spend the entire allotted time on each site, but I also got used to clicking the "Ignore Limit for Today" button at the bottom of the pop-up. Before I knew it, half an hour of scrolling would stretch into a full hour, then two hours.

Though you can always opt to set rigid time limits or delete certain apps for good, "ninety-eight percent of people won't do it," says therapist William Schroeder. Not only is online abstinence tough to maintain, it's not practical if you depend on the platforms to function at work or want to stay in touch with family. Online pacing tactics are most successful when they fit into your life's existing rhythms rather than subverting them.

Creating Rules of Engagement

Though perpetual digital retreats often aren't realistic, setting clear terms of engagement—deciding how you want to participate in online spaces and why—can help you set a measured pace in a virtual world designed to fracture your focus at every turn.

It's easy to fall into a mindless content-consumption cycle that upends your best-laid plans; that's the very cycle the online world is set up to encourage. But when you shift away from consumption and move toward directed learning and contribution, you give yourself a natural opening to disengage once you've achieved what you set out to do. You move toward establishing your own, more deliberate rhythms, rather than letting online notifications and algorithms dictate your pace.

During one of my chats with Amy Baltzell, I unload about how entrenched my digital habits have become. Like just about everyone else on social media, I get drawn into hypnotic sequences of short videos, but I also engage in dead-end debates against my better judgment. I'll post about something that's happening in the world, see the replies roll in, and get caught up in responding to critics—a cycle not unlike the ludic-loop trance of watching one reel after another. "Probably it would have been better if I never got into that discussion in the first place," I tell Baltzell. "When I look back at how many hours I've put down that particular well, it's scary."

Baltzell pauses. "Has there ever been a time that you've been in a back-and-forth and you feel like it's had a positive impact?"

"I think there has," I say. "But it hasn't been a huge positive impact. What kind of change did it bring about? Not much."

"If you pull back to the thirty-thousand-mile view," Baltzell continues, "is it a good use of your time to be engaged in social media? I don't know what you're going for, but to be clear, what is it you're going for? What's the impact you want to have?"

Our exchange gets me thinking along more pragmatic lines. I might tell myself I'm going online to connect with interesting people, but am I actually there for anything beyond the dopamine rush? I want to share little-known stories and insights that will jolt readers out of complacency and prompt thoughtful discussions. But I consume far more content than I generate. Too often, I wade in, grab onto the algorithmic towrope, and wait to see where it pulls me.

Since then, my attempts at more deliberate engagement have been far from absolute. I still indulge in cake-decorating videos and 140-character news blasts on occasion. But I'm also posting at least once a week on issues I've spent time thinking about. Some of these in-depth posts, like one about the demonization of Haitian immigrants to the United States, generate the kind of hopeful discussion I hope to spark—a positive groundswell that motivates me to keep sharing along similar lines.

When I just want to zone out or kill time, I toggle over to an internet rabbit hole that *isn't* Facebook or Instagram: the Internet Archive's collection of out-of-print books. I've been chewing through a few extra books a month on Internet Archive, much to my own surprise, and some of what I read inspires new story ideas. Replacing one compelling habit with another, studies show, often works better than banishing the first habit.

For other people setting clearer intentions about how to spend their online time, those objectives often help them streamline their use in ways that don't involve imposing limits. "I've curated my social feeds so that I only follow accounts that align with my goals," says Montrez Williams, an entrepreneur and marketing consultant based in Boston. After weeding out the clutter and seeking out other posters he aspires to be like—

scrappy entrepreneurs with integrity—he's found himself going down fewer online rabbit holes, and by reaching out to people whose work he admires, he's found several long-term mentors.

This kind of intentional engagement trumps constraint because, while imposed limits often lead us to rebel or tune out, we're more motivated to act in ways that reinforce our desired identities. In a University of Houston study, participants who told themselves "I can't eat unhealthy snacks" chose chocolate over a granola bar nearly twice as often as those who reasoned, "I *don't* eat unhealthy snacks." While the former group was tempted to defy what they saw as a restriction, the latter group viewed eating well as part of their identity—something they would want to do even if no one else was watching.

That result helps explain why principled online refusal seems to work better than hard-and-fast time limits. Instead of telling yourself *I can't go on TikTok for more than an hour a day*, embrace clear self-definition instead: *I don't stay on TikTok for more than an hour a day. I have other, higher priorities.*

Though tech companies have grown adept at monopolizing (and monetizing) people's attention, stepping into a self-chosen identity requires you to channel that attention elsewhere, meaning there's less available for the feed creators to feast on.

You can also draw on what captivates you to plan deliberate habit swaps. Rather than willing yourself to stay off Instagram after lunch, plan to polish the poems you've been working on or touch base with mentors who share your interest in childhood literacy. (If you've completed Ben Rogers's re-storying exercise in chapter 3, your notes may help you zero in on what new habits are likely to feel most meaningful.) "I stopped looking at my phone," Jenny Odell writes, "because I was looking at something else, something so absorbing that I couldn't turn away." Whatever they are for you, such absorbing pursuits serve as springboards into long-term flourishing.

Retreat and Recommitment

While streamlining your online intentions helps you set a sustainable digital pace in the long run, planned shorter retreats can serve as a kind of pacing reset, clearing more space for what allows you to flourish outside the online world. When Noelle Frost resolved to spend the month of January away from social media, she found herself cooking more and taking long hikes. Though she loved both activities, they'd gotten short shrift when social media claimed so much of her attention, and her life felt more balanced when she dove back into them.

Still, Frost discovered total abstinence wasn't practical for long. Being out of the online loop meant she was out of the loop in real life more often than she'd expected. During her fast, she missed out on a number of events she would have liked to attend. She also lost the thread of Facebook group discussions about her local community.

When you accept that you're eventually going to re-engage, periodic fasts create opportunities to reflect on how you'll spend future online time. Once John Green re-engaged with social media after his yearlong break, he began cutting a more intentional swath. During a recent World Cup, he posted a series of TikToks aimed at helping people appreciate the complexity and beauty of soccer. He's also made YouTube videos to build awareness of the dangers of tuberculosis, hoping to help lower the cost of drugs for treating the disease. His online posts reflected and furthered the kind of changes he wanted to create. "This is the middle of history," Green told MSNBC commentator Chris Hayes, describing the global battle against tuberculosis. "And what our job is, what falls to us, is to write a better end." Time after time, research shows, it's precisely this kind of meaningful engagement that drives flourishing.

The best digital pacers, then, aren't completely abstinent—not forever, anyway. Like shrewd pacers in other domains, they're more like marathoners who set clear goals and do periodic sanity checks to make sure they're on course to reach those goals.

While online retreats can give you time and space to refine your goals for online engagement, you can also build sanity checks into your normal routine by setting customized alerts that pop up before you launch into addictive scrolling—messages like "What am I getting out of being online?" or "Who do I want to touch base with today?" (Apps like Screen-Zen offer one way to set these kinds of alerts.) Unlike pre-set online time limits you'll only try to override, alert messages remind you of what you actually value and what you want to do with your time online. They cultivate an awareness that steers you toward focused activity and subsequent disengagement.

Reclaiming Your Time

Our collective desire to disengage could ultimately make digital pacing less of an uphill battle. In the past few years, online fatigue has mounted. Fewer creators are now feeding the kinds of content streams that draw eyeballs, resulting in flatter, more cookie-cutter content. (You might have sensed this if you've ever watched a dozen reels end to end and barely recalled what any were about.) And a tidal wave of so-called AI slop—autogenerated content optimized to drive engagement—has left us all less sure if the pablum that populates our feeds was even created by humans.

At the same time, communities are springing up to support healthier kinds of online participation. There are old-school message boards, where posts appear in the order they were made and not in order of popularity, and there are also semi-private discussion forums like Slack, where people can discuss movies, books, or music without following an algorithm's lead.

In light of those shifts, it's not surprising that people spent ten fewer minutes on social media each day in late 2024 than they did two years earlier—a notable dip, since it followed such ferocious growth trends. And in a reprise of twentieth-century standoffs against Big Tobacco, lawmakers are taking steps to regulate social media companies' addictive offerings. In New York State, kids can no longer view algorithm-driven social feeds without their parents' permission, and similar legislation has started making its way through Congress.

Could more contracture be ahead, the way a star's collapse accelerates after a certain point? It's hard to imagine full implosion, given how many of our meetings and exchanges happen in the online world. Yet freedom from the ludic loop now seems more within reach than it was years ago—and the more the loop's attentional tyranny fades, the easier it becomes to turn to what enriches us outside it. This attentional shift has its own protective pacing effect: The more actual fulfillment you tap into, the less need you'll have for the digital facsimiles that are constantly on offer.

After her monthlong fast, Noelle Frost returned to Facebook and Instagram, just as she'd known she would. Since her time away, she's gotten better at noticing her social media absorption before it takes full hold. "About the middle of the afternoon of my workday, I might check Instagram, just kind of as a mental break, or right before I go to bed at night." If she finds herself refreshing the page at other times, she asks herself what else she could be doing. Mulling over other priorities helps motivate her to log off, keeping her out of the ludic loop.

To maintain her new long-term digital pace, Frost is planning regular January social media breaks, a way of making sure the platforms' hold on her never grows strong enough to choke off everything else. She knows the break will create space for what helps her to flourish: blitzing through her to-read pile, catching up with friends, or taking wilderness hikes— and she also knows those shifted priorities will persist after the fast has ended. "It's just a matter of, *How do I want to spend my time?*"

Chapter 7

Flourishing in Flow

Alannah Yip chalked her hands, took a final deep breath, and prepared to mount the wall at the 2020 Pan-American Continental Championships in Los Angeles. This was her chance to qualify for the Tokyo Olympic Games in sport climbing.

Instead of trying to stay limber with warmup exercises, Yip deliberately turned her energy inward. In the minutes before her climb, she lay down, trying to conserve her resources, and focused on the airflow in and out of her lungs. When she finally rose to mount the wall, she was acutely conscious of the sensation of her feet on the ground.

As Yip moved from one climbing grip to the next, it felt as if her arms and legs were moving of their own accord. She wasn't second-guessing her instincts about where to grab and how to balance; she'd attained a state of mental flow, moving through the course without getting in her own way. "My body was moving my body," she remembers. "My brain was definitely thinking, but it was almost separate."

Hardly anyone who was watching Yip glide across the wall knew how much inner preparation had gone into this moment. In some competitions, the bigger the moment, the more pressure she'd felt to live up to others' expectations. But here, in one of the biggest competitions of her life, Yip's self-consciousness dropped away.

The focus she'd honed leading up to the competition took on its own momentum, as she shifted effortlessly from the handhold before her to the one just above it. This state of single-minded engagement, which researcher Mihaly Csikszentmihalyi termed "flow," is one that "leads to a sense of ecstasy, a sense of clarity," as Csikszentmihalyi explained before his death in 2021. "You know exactly what you want to do from one moment to the other." Studies show a high degree of connection between different brain regions during flow, which helps explain its singular intensity.

In the years since Csikszentmihalyi's insights went viral, optimizers and executives alike have branded flow as a flume ride to superhuman efficiency. The human relations firm McLean & Company offers managers a detailed road map for activating flow, promising it will "enable employees to achieve optimal results, increasing engagement, performance, and productivity." Influencers like Jim Kwik echo this message, racking up tens of thousands of views with videos like "Flow State: Unlock Your Superhuman Productivity."

Framed in this way, flow looks like just another enticement to keep up the hustle. However, those who tout flow as a productivity hack fundamentally misjudge its power.

When you have the right focus, some experts suggest, flow can help you blitz through nearly any challenge you face. But this take is misleading. Years of research suggest that only certain kinds of tasks reliably induce flow. Not only do they need to be challenging, taking you to the edge of your capacities, but they should also be pursuits that engage you in and of themselves.

What makes flow integral to a well-paced life isn't just that it lets you get more done in less time, though sometimes it does. It's that flow leads you deeper into pursuits that not only build your daily resilience but help you flourish in the long run.

Though some productivity experts view flow as a form of mastery that begets achievement, the true power of flow becomes evident when practitioners rise above the self and give themselves over to a task outside of it. Whether that task relates to what they do for a living is irrelevant. Untethered from typical achievement benchmarks, flow becomes its own reward, allowing for deep engagement with something beyond the self—the very definition of flourishing. "When you're in flow," the violinist Diane Allen says, "your work refuels you."

The Productivity-Hack Myth

Long before Mihaly Csikszentmihalyi understood what flow was, it imbued his chaotic childhood with order and meaning. Before he was ten years old, Csikszentmihalyi saw friends and family members killed in World War II, and soon afterward, the Hungarian government revoked his family's citizenship and expelled them from the country. Amid the chaos, Csikszentmihalyi stayed even-keeled by absorbing himself in demanding pursuits—and intuiting a link between those immersive escapes and his well-being.

One of Csikszentmihalyi's uncles taught him to play chess when he was nine, which stood out as his first experience in "moving into a separate reality, temporarily." The game offered solace and distraction, blotting out memories of wartime traumas. After he learned to climb rocks, those moments of absorption returned when he made his way up sheer cliff faces. Climbing, he told a writer, gave him "a feeling that you were doing everything you could, that your whole being was involved, and that you forgot everything else."

Later, after Csikszentmihalyi became a psychologist, he heard about a group of weavers in northern Italy who worked in the same way their ancestors had for centuries. Each family member would run the looms, designing their own intricate weaving patterns, until they grew tired. At that point, they would stop to let another weaver take a turn.

What surprised Csikszentmihalyi was that most family members named weaving as their favorite activity, ahead of going to clubs, vacationing, or watching TV. This joyful work reminded Csikszentmihalyi of his own transcendent moments of focus while rock climbing or playing chess.

Around the world, the people Csikszentmihalyi studied reported striking similarities in their flow experiences. When they entered flow, they usually had a clear, challenging goal in mind, whether it was completing a report, finishing a race, or solving a puzzle. And as they became immersed in flow, they relinquished control, feeling as if the flow's current were spiriting them along. They also felt a kind of joy that had nothing to do with achievement in the typical sense. "The ego falls away. Time flies. Every action, movement, and thought follows inevitably from the previous one," Csikszentmihalyi reflected in one interview. "You're using your skills to the utmost."

But once the flow concept entered public awareness, it wasn't long before corporate ladder climbers seized on the concept as a way to do more in less time. Their claim was based on a grain of truth; studies had found, after all, that some people reported getting more done faster when they were in flow.

Productivity mavens, however, soon redefined flow as a kind of cheat code to hyper-charge overall efficiency, promising they'd be able to use flow to finish a day's work in less than half the time they normally would. "With a little bit of effort," podcaster and consultant Sam Spurlin writes, "you can find more flow in everything you do."

But flow isn't some magical power-up you can use to propel yourself through processing Slack messages, doing your taxes, or making calls you dread. What promoters often overlook are the conditions that research shows are necessary to maintain flow.

First, the work you're tackling needs to hit a cognitive sweet spot: It must be challenging enough to demand all your concentration, but not so challenging that you're tempted to give up after a short time. Second, the task should be what researchers call "intrinsically motivating," or compelling in and of itself—ideally, something you'd do for fun anyway. Since studies find that people enter flow more readily when they do things they actually enjoy, trying to use flow as a catchall productivity hack is counterproductive. "If you dread a task," writes *The Habit Guide* author Leo Babauta, "you'll have a hard time losing yourself in it."

Flow, Ego Erasure, and Flourishing

It's easy to spin flow as a way to win the one-upmanship game, a shortcut to achieving more than anyone else in less time. But this take is precisely backward. From a neurological standpoint, flow is an antidote to the kind of egotism that compels you to grind well past your limits. In short, flow makes you forget yourself in ways that are profoundly freeing.

When neuroscientist Charles Limb and his colleagues scanned the brains of improv jazz musicians as they noodled around on the keyboard—a quintessential flow pursuit—they noticed that activity plummeted in large swaths of the brain's dorsolateral prefrontal cortex, which helps govern self-monitoring. It appeared that, like Alannah Yip at the Olympic trials, the musicians weren't burning much mental energy worrying about how good their performance was. Instead, they were narrowing their vision to the present, focusing on its moment-to-moment demands.

This mental state gives rise to a feeling of surrender, as if a force larger than yourself is at work. Flow feels like a peak experience in part because it blots out self-awareness the same way spiritual immersion does. When people are in flow, their brains' dopaminergic reward systems also grow more active, generating pleasure and fulfillment.

As she ascended the wall in Los Angeles, Alannah Yip inched closer to this kind of transcendent immersion. She swung effortlessly from one handhold to the next, unconcerned with assessing her progress. Partway through the climb, she stood on a long black platform to focus her mind. "It's important to stop for a second, take some deep breaths, make sure my brain is not running away and snowballing," she says. At that point in the course, she told herself, "Okay, a couple more moves."

Toward the end of her climb, Yip got so deeply into flow that—without pausing to question herself—she skipped grabbing a handhold that was right in front of her, something she rarely does. Yet her split-second decision somehow felt exactly right. "I just looked at that hold and was, like, 'No, I don't need to grab that.'" Spectators picked up on just how dialed-in Yip had become. One broadcast commentator pointed out that she looked more comfortable in the upper section of the course, even though parts of it were more difficult.

A few handholds later, it was official: "Alannah Yip has set a new high point here," the commentator exulted. "She's going to the Olympic Games!"

Though Yip's body shook with exhaustion, she also felt recharged, inspired for the new challenges ahead. She was elated that she'd managed to forget herself despite outside pressures, transforming what could have been a Sisyphean task into a playful experiment. "When you find the flow state, you're moving intuitively," she says. "You feel like you're flowing with the rock, with the wall. You're more creative in the ways you move and figure things out. And that's a really powerful feeling."

Transcendent moments like Yip's refute hustle-culture notions that Herculean self-control is what fuels success. A surer route to flourishing is ego erasure—the kind that regularly happens in flow. The more you forget yourself when you're immersed in flow, the happier, more energized and purposeful you feel. In this way, flow stints confer psychological benefits that make them integral to a well-paced life, regardless of what you accomplish (or don't) during them.

While self-focused achieverdom sets you up for wild pace shifts between overdrive and exhaustion, the self-transcendence that happens in flow dictates a different rhythm—one in which joy and engagement, not a fear of being surpassed, propel you along.

Finding Transcendent Flow

Concert violinist, speaker, and author Diane Allen aims to help people venture further into the kind of transcendent flow that fuels long-term flourishing. From childhood onward, Allen craved what she called "getting into the music," becoming so absorbed in playing her instrument that nothing else mattered. At that point, she had no idea what flow was. All she knew was that getting into the music made playing feel easy and exhilarating.

When she became a professional violinist, Allen grew adept at finding that feeling whenever she went on stage—and she found ways to "get into the music" outside the performance realm as well. One time, she applied for a violin teaching job at a local school, and when she showed up for the interview, an unexpected crowd awaited her: students, parents, musicians, other teachers, and even a local conductor.

Having applied for the job on a whim, Allen hadn't prepared all that much for the interview, so she decided to fling herself into it without any expectations. That decision turned out to be freeing. As Allen answered students' questions and refined their technique, she wasn't worrying about what those students or evaluators thought of her. Like Yip on the Olympic Trials wall, she was simply tuned in to the demands of the moment. When the interview wrapped up, she was shocked to realize just how much time had passed. "I just rocked it," she says. "At the end of the day, they hired me on the spot."

Later, when Allen tried to describe such immersive, joyful moments to friends, one replied, "Well, you're talking about the flow state, right?"

Finding out that "getting into the music" had a name was a revelation for Allen, and she started developing ways to help others capture the quality of joyful attention she'd perfected over the years. That joyful attention had helped her pace herself through a multi-decade performing career. Though intense, demanding days sometimes depleted her energy, she soon bounced back, fueled by her passion for getting into the musical flow.

Allen approached her newest mission like a practitioner, not a researcher. "The way I talk about flow is like a flow for the people," she says. "I want to reawaken it within them, because we all have the capacity for it."

These days, Allen travels around the country both physically and virtually, helping a wide range of clients develop their flow practice. The training system she developed, which she calls "Flow Strategy," revolves around reverse engineering. Since nearly everyone has had at least a fleeting glimpse of the flow state, she asks people to remember a specific time they experienced it. For example, if you're a chef, you might have found flow when you were perfecting a new dish. If you're a scientist, you might have found it while combing through genetic test results, searching for hidden patterns in the data.

Allen stresses that what gets you into flow may have nothing at all to do with your day job. It can be anything you enjoy that is also challenging. "For one person, it's going to be getting lost in an Excel spreadsheet," she says. "Somebody else will be in the garage fixing a motorcycle."

Whatever the flow-promoting activity, it should stretch you just a hair past your current abilities, since tasks that are difficult (but not *too* difficult) are most conducive to flow. If you're trying something totally out of your wheelhouse—say, writing a computer program when you don't know how to code—you'll struggle to get into flow because the work you put into it will produce scant results. But if you're operating at the edge of your capacity in a domain you know well, that sustained effort will yield clear progress that keeps flow going.

Once you've figured out what induces flow for you, try replicating the specific conditions that helped you get into flow in the past. This process, too, is highly personal. It might mean sitting at the same desk each morning, going through a specific pre-workout warmup, or firing up a certain playlist when you head out to do some garage tinkering. It could even be as simple as heading to a room or space you've designated for work (even a closet or well-hidden corner, if that's all you have to spare).

It's also crucial to think about what makes a flow-promoting activity meaningful to you, Allen says. Do you like creating spreadsheets because, by doing so, you're creating clarity and order? Do you like playing music because you're fueling joy and unity? Once you've figured out what gives you a flow-promoting sense of purpose, you can use that knowledge to find flow in other meaningful settings. If you love working on mathematical formulas because they create clarity, you can access flow during a keynote talk by reminding yourself that your speech, too, is a chance to offer clarity.

Though the specifics of your flow routine matter, your commitment to creating it matters just as much. "If you can define it, you can replicate it," Allen says. "And then the more you practice it, the more automatic it becomes."

To establish a mental flow groove, your practice needs to be regular. Steven Kotler, executive director of the Flow Research Collective, advises setting aside a ninety-minute stretch at least once a week to delve into your chosen pursuit.

These longer stretches are necessary because flow often takes its time picking up momentum. In his conception of the "Breakout Principle," former Harvard cardiologist and mind-body expert Herbert Benson noted that people moving toward flow tend to have a "struggle" phase at the outset, when they're most prone to distraction. In part, that's because brain areas responsible for self-monitoring and critique rarely quiet down right away. It's also because facing a challenge is stressful, triggering the release of fight-or-flight hormones that can stymie single-minded focus. The relaxed state that enables flow begins only after this initial burst of stress and self-critique has passed. (This helps explain why the optimizer approach of wedging demanding tasks into fifteen- or twenty-minute stretches—say, writing a novel page by page on your train commute—rarely works as well as advertised.)

As you launch into longer stretches of concentration, you can reduce your mental static by paring back the number of distractions around you. The more fractured your focus, Czikszentmihalyi points out, the harder it gets to enter sustained flow, especially when the distractions aren't related to your primary focus (keeping an Instagram chat window open while you're trying to write a paper).

When I try Allen's reverse-engineering approach to finding flow—re-creating the conditions that have led to it in the past—I realize I was often away from home when I really got going on a creative project, whether at a coffee shop, library, or college quad. (I did one memorable stretch of book drafting at a neighborhood taqueria.) Much of the time, I also switched off my internet connection before getting down to work.

Re-creating these conditions ushers in more successful flow attempts, just as Allen would predict. I get into flow with my writing more reliably when I leave home or cut myself off from the online realm. Yet neither of these conditions, as I discover, guarantee that flow will take hold. From time to time, getting into flow feels easy, as though I'm letting a current carry me along. Other days, as I click frantically between news updates and Temu.com, flow feels as unattainable as an Olympic berth.

At the outset of my work, I usually face the "struggle phase" Herbert Benson described, flailing around for between fifteen minutes and half an hour. Just when my thoughts seem to be coalescing, they disperse like a cloud of no-see-ums, and I have to fight the temptation to toggle back to social media.

Yet if I'm lucky, a transition occurs in somewhere between a half hour and an hour—so subtle that I don't recognize it at first. My focus narrows and my surroundings—the worktable, the skyline view out my window—drop away, just as the crowds did for Yip in Los Angeles. The unsettled energy of the previous half hour inverts, turning suction-like in its intensity.

When I emerge from my flow state a couple of hours later, I feel surprisingly energized, even though my concentration is starting to flag. I'm still caught up in the rush of propulsive energy, a current that keeps drawing me back into the evolving essay. Though I give myself permission to detach, I keep returning to my document to polish a sloppy sentence, sharpen a metaphor, clarify a concept. It feels impossible to pull away—but I'm okay with that, because, at this particular moment, I wouldn't want to be anywhere else.

Flow for the Long Haul

My own trials give me a clearer sense of flow's most profound benefit: how it helps you set a sustaining pace free of locked-in productivity benchmarks. Diane Allen doesn't aim to "get into the music" because she thinks it'll make her five times faster at practicing. She does it because flow brings her a sense of joy and purpose that has propelled her through the ups and downs of a lifelong career.

Other longtime flow practitioners have a similar take. The elation of zeroing in on what they most want to pursue, whether it's work-related or not, makes each week's inevitable stress and drudgery less draining. For years, online learning expert Randall Tinfow has guarded what he calls his "cloistered time," when he shuts himself in a tiny room from 4:30 to 7:00 a.m.—no food, email, or social media allowed—to focus on his creative projects. Tinfow's wife once asked him, "If you had to give up either sex or your cloistered time, what would you choose?" When Tinfow found himself unable to answer, she grinned and said, "Yeah, I figured that!"

Habitual flow stints also elevate your overall energy levels in unexpected ways. After linguist Martina Cola started reserving sixty to ninety minutes a day for intense focus on her research, she noticed she felt better and more fired up the rest of the day, ready to rise to new challenges.

That energy burst may stem from flow-related dopamine activity, which can elevate well-being and tamp down fatigue. In one Taiwanese study of eighty-four full-time employees, those who entered flow during the workday reported feeling more energetic by the end than those who didn't achieve flow states.

But Martina Cola also attributes her energy lift to her heightened ability to summon calm concentration during her favorite projects—an ability that Steven Kotler notes can emerge through regular flow practice.

"Before, I easily got tired, irritated, and bored," Cola says. "Now it's like there's some sense of stability." The mental stability flow allows her to keep a steady pace throughout the week, no matter what unfolds. Cola now feels grounded enough to meet each day's challenges as they arise, rather than getting lost in the extremes of procrastination or overwork.

Cola's experience mirrors that of people who channeled flow during the COVID pandemic. College students who regularly got into flow during lockdowns continued to flourish even though so much of what happened around them was out of their control. They felt more engaged in their day-to-day pursuits and saw their lives as more meaningful.

The Virtuous Flow Cycle

At first, flow's energizing effects can seem like a license to toil endlessly, as if flow, like a solar panel, could keep all systems running at near-zero cost. But as exhilarating as flow can be, it's still physically exhausting, subject to natural human limits. Since flow can never become a perpetual motion machine, practitioners must balance the flow ethos of total immersion with stretches of rest and disengagement.

While Mihaly Csikszentmihalyi went so far as to suggest that fatigue goes away when people find flow, this claim feels too glib; it elides the reality that the body and mind tire no matter how absorbing the activity. Even when it feels effortless, flow demands intense cognitive effort, meaning you need to follow it with downtime just as you would if you'd run a race. After a couple of hours spent in flow, it's natural to feel tapped out enough to need a long break. Writer Ernest Hemingway understood the value of backing away after focused work stints. "I had learned already never to empty the well," he wrote, "but always stop when there was still something there in the deep part of the well, and let it refill at night from the springs that fed it."

Yet flow's long-term buoying effects are equally significant. There's the feeling of exhilaration when the undertow first gets hold of you, the ecstasy Diane Allen associates with "getting into the music." More enduring, however, are the broader kinds of renewal the flow sets in motion. Not only do flow stints feed life satisfaction, but flow can help keep you on an even keel as chaos unfolds around you.

What researchers haven't been able to pin down, at least not yet, is another intriguing development Allen and others report in their flow practice. When Diane Allen gets into flow consistently, she says, she enters a kind of virtuous cycle: Her flow prowess improves her performance, which in turn deepens her flow state, heightening her performance still more. When she was immersed in a flow-promoting gig—working closely with a skilled Oregon conductor—not only was she supremely happy, she also reached a new pinnacle of musicianship. "The more I got into the music, the better I played. The better I played, the more I got into the music," she says. "That's the positive feedback loop." So, too, for

Alannah Yip, whose flow states propel her through ever-tougher climbing feats, spurring deeper focus and joy.

This virtuous cycle shows how flow can help you set a sustaining pace that has nothing to do with productivity as commonly defined. Grind culture is about muscling through, defeating the original sin of sloth, elevating the self by wrestling it into submission. Flow practice approaches human nature not with hostility but with deep curiosity. It guides you to build more of what energizes and engrosses you into your life's architecture, whether it's writing innovative code, counseling those in need, or scaling sheer walls. Flow is additive rather than subtractive or punitive; it underscores and refines what makes you most yourself, replenishing reserves drawn down by years of overwork. For strivers who have chased external benchmarks their entire adult lives, it's a homecoming in the very best sense.

Chapter 8

Brief Candles

When Kurt Stange was a full-time family doctor in Cleveland, Ohio, he rarely had much wiggle room in his day. Given his fast-paced schedule, Stange could be forgiven for embracing the speed dictum that dominates medicine: examining each patient as soon as they arrive, recommending a clear course of action, and briskly ushering in the next patient. For hospitals and clinics, this is the approach that yields the maximum possible returns, at least on paper.

But Stange—now a professor at Case Western Reserve University's Center for Community Health Integration—has taken a different route, relating to patients in ways that defy medicine's tightening focus on efficiency. He listens carefully when they're talking about their symptoms, but also when they mention other aspects of their lives: milestone events, challenging relationships, job setbacks. And because he pays close attention to their answers, the conversation often evolves in directions he couldn't have predicted. During these exchanges, linear time ceases to have as much meaning for Stange as he considers how to serve their needs—some physical, others more existential.

A number of years ago, one of Stange's patients was struggling with repetitive stress injuries she'd gotten on the job. While Stange chatted with her, she opened up, confiding that her employers were trying to push her out because of her disability. In continued conversations, Stange came to appreciate how threatened the patient felt, so he filed sequences of paperwork that would protect her if her bosses tried to cut her loose.

A while later, Stange got a call from that same patient, who was agitated and breathless. She was irate at a work supervisor who had offended her. She was also upset because she'd gone out to buy a gun, and the store had told her she had to wait three days before making a purchase. Stange's antennae immediately went up. "I said, 'Why don't you come in now? Let's talk a little bit.'"

After Stange and his patient spoke for a few moments, it grew clear that she'd been making plans to shoot people at her workplace. Stange talked her down and made sure she got the help she needed. "She wanted me to do that, I think," Stange says. He understood, too, that if it weren't for the moments of undivided attention he'd offered beforehand—chatting with her about work struggles, filling out each disability form that crossed his desk—he might never have had the chance to intervene.

Within a few minutes, Kurt Stange shifted the course of his patient's life and his own in ways that would endure for years. Such moments of undivided selfless attention, which I call "brief candles," resonate in ways that far outlast their duration. Some brief candles are subtle moments whose impact accrues through repetition, while others create dramatic transformations that alter the initiator's path as well as the recipient's. And the first type of brief candle sometimes lights the way for the second.

Brief candles upend an assumption that guides so many pacing decisions: that the amount of time you invest determines your returns. We often approach pacing our lives as if we're balancing an equation, where adding to one side means subtracting from the other side in equal measure. If you volunteer on weekends, you'll have less time to recover from a busy week. If you spend an hour on Zoom with a friend, you sacrifice an hour of focused deep work.

Brief candles defy this zero-sum model. Though they take little time or schedule shuffling, these moments are integral to shrewd pacing, setting up everyone involved for long-term flourishing. What best predicts people's health and happiness, decades-long studies have found, is the on-going quality of their relationships. Brief candles create bonds that sustain those who ignite the glow as well as those who receive it. And when everyday rushing and chaos obscure your purposeful goals, brief candles can re-illuminate them. While William Shakespeare famously described life itself as a brief candle, one destined to wink out, lighting brief candles for others gives you a kind of immortality that burns brighter as the flame is passed along.

Though brief candles might seem elusive, you can generate more of them by priming yourself to seek them out and absorb their significance. Doing so changes your brain in measurable ways. The rewards of lighting brief candles can motivate you to continue the practice, orienting you toward a life like Kurt Stange's—one whose impact surpasses anything grit alone could coax into being.

A Focused Beam

Brief candles are not exchanges of time for something else of equal value. Nor are they networking ploys, apparent favors that are really calculated deposits with an assumed rate of return. In fact, brief candles stubbornly resist being quantified at all; they are untethered from time, space, and ultimate results. They are offered gratis, for the recipient to use as they will.

What most differentiates brief candles from ordinary interactions is the quality of attention the bearer brings to the encounter. This kind of attention—akin to what psychologist Carl Rogers called "active listening"—stems from wanting to inhabit someone else's perspective.

At the heart of this attention is a single-pointed focus on the other person, a focus you can hone by asking open-ended questions ("Can you tell me more about why you're stressed?") or reflecting back what they are saying ("It sounds like you hate work because your coworker is claiming credit for what you do. Is that right?").

While this kind of focus is demanding to sustain, the architecture of our bodies and minds supports it. Just as we're built to withstand brief periods of stress, we're built for brief, white-hot stretches of attention.

The humans who thrived in ancestral times weren't necessarily the ones with the most doggedness or endurance; they were the ones who paid attention at the right times. That remains true today. In a study of preschool-aged children, the least-stressed kids were the ones who had caregivers giving them the most focused attention, not the ones who invested the most time. Garry Landreth, founder of the University of North Texas Center for Play Therapy, often advises parents to give kids "thirty-second bursts of attention," putting aside everything they're doing to focus solely on what their child needs.

People who sense others are paying close attention to them show high levels of activity in the ventral striatum, a brain area that processes rewarding experiences. Not only does this kind of attention feel gratifying but people also grow to admire those who offer it—and may be more open to adopting the giver's perspectives.

Skilled attention givers can trigger profound inner shifts even in those who enter their lives for only a short time. When I was a child, a family friend named Geoff Lister often came to dinner at our house. Every time, without fail, he would ask me what I'd been writing about or what books I'd been reading and what I liked about them.

I doubt most of these chats lasted more than a few minutes. Yet they made a deep impression on me in ways that defied their length. I had rarely been in dialogue with anyone else who felt so completely present, so tuned in to what I was saying, and who so deeply conveyed that it mattered. My parents listened to me plenty, and we had long, in-depth conversations. Still—fairly or not—I believed they had to do so because I was their kid, because I was biologically part of them, and they me.

Geoff's talks with me, on the other hand, were gifts of undivided attention freely given. Geoff could easily have exchanged a few pleasantries with me and my brother, and left us to our own devices. Plenty of adults did. It was the natural order of things.

The gap between what was required and what Geoff had given me propelled me back to our conversations at times when I doubted I had anything to contribute. Those unexpected brief candles, consistently offered, helped me trust myself as a writer and thinker, shaping the course of my career in ways that helped me flourish. They multiplied after the initial gift in ways neither Geoff nor I could have predicted.

Kindling Long-Term Meaning

In his decades as a primary-care physician, Kurt Stange came to appreciate the way brief candles endure after months or years have passed. When Stange meets a new patient, he tries to treat each such visit as the start of a long relationship. He relates to patients in ways that have little to do with efficiency, asking about their kids, their careers, what their lives are about. And when they return to see him again, as many do, he revisits those earlier openings, asking if they've had any luck with their job search or whether they've tried to quit smoking.

Such moments of focused attention, Stange notes, helped kick off his own career. When Stange was a high school freshman, his biology teacher, Miss Kunzog, took an interest in him and asked if he'd like to take pictures for the school yearbook. He took Miss Kunzog up on her offer—and while he soon ruled out photography as a profession, he realized that the biology he was learning from Miss Kunzog fired his imagination. If not for that initial brief candle she'd lit, he might have ended up in a different place.

Stange has also recognized how such everyday, low-key encounters create the kind of trust that allows him to light life-changing brief candles. He knows he never would have been able to talk his patient out of pulling out a gun at work had it not been for the succession of office visits beforehand—the ones where he paid attention to her fears, her goals, and the obstacles he could help her surmount.

Similarly, he has found he can help people better navigate life-or-death decisions when he has a clearer idea of who they are as human beings. Through the sequence of brief candles he lights, he comes to know his patients well and to understand their values: how much they prize comfort over longevity, how much (or little) they trust high-risk treatments. This foundation of trust makes it easier for him to level with them—to say, for instance, "You could do another chemo round, but it may not work, and you might want to spend that time with your family," thereby starting the kinds of conversations that support their quality of life for months or years to come.

Part of what's helped Stange keep a sustainable pace for decades, amid record levels of medical burnout, are the moments when he grasps how he's altered a patient's trajectory—sometimes in ways that impact even more lives. Once you start paying attention, Stange says, you recognize the abiding value of doing so. "It gives meaning to our work."

No insurance provider reimburses for modes of attention that have little to do with diagnosis or treatment. But for practitioners who don't cultivate this kind of attention, work becomes "just delivering one commodity after another," Stange says. "It's not that satisfying after a while."

When psychiatrists at Harvard University studied the life trajectories of more than one hundred people, they found that those who cultivated what they called "generativity" in midlife—a concern for guiding others, including members of the next generation—were more likely to flourish in their later years, enjoying better mental and cognitive health.

Lighting brief candles, then, is a sound long-term pacing strategy as well as an altruistic venture. Though grind culture promises status and rapid accumulation, these pale next to the returns of focused contribution: adding your own verse, as Walt Whitman might put it, to a vast and powerful play.

Seeking Out Brief Candles

Yet as Stange knows, it's challenging to introduce brief candles on command. They involve a kind of pas de deux between the offerer and the recipient. If either party is out of sorts or out of step, no spark will kindle.

What you can do is prime yourself to notice brief-candle opportunities—and make the most of them when they arise. "Attention is motivated," says Rick Hanson, a psychologist at UC Berkeley's Greater Good Science Center. "What are we leaning toward, and are we looking for the candles?"

Psychologist Zeno Franco has found that considering what you'll do in situations that call for thoughtful intervention helps prepare you to take action when these situations arise. In the same way, it's easier to light brief candles when you've considered the particulars of how you might do so, sketching out ahead of time which situations might call for them and how you'll respond.

As you formulate your plan, think about times someone intervened for you in ways that turned out to have a major impact. What did that intervention look like? Was it a recommendation that came through at just the right time? Or a conversation that affirmed your potential when you didn't see a way forward? How might you be able to emulate those approaches in your own daily encounters?

Reflecting on your highest intentions can also prime you to look for brief candles. Those skilled at seizing brief-candle opportunities, like former school principal Joe DeMarsh, often develop shortcut modes of calling their values to mind.

Though decades have passed, California nephrologist George Ting has never forgotten a brief candle DeMarsh lit when Ting was a student at the American School in Japan. DeMarsh spotted Ting—then an impoverished young immigrant—slipping a few dollars out of a purse in an empty classroom. Terrified, Ting thought he'd be suspended, ending his chances of going to a top college. But DeMarsh, knowing Ting's potential and sensing his deep regret, let him walk free with six words: "You can do better than that." Ting went on to thrive at Columbia University and ascend to the top of his field. "The chance he gave me," Ting would later say of DeMarsh, "catapulted me into the rest of my life."

After DeMarsh died, his wife's daughter Sam Childs said that for as long as she could remember, DeMarsh had kept a piece of paper in his wallet, refolded so many times it was fraying at the edges. On the paper was a quote frequently attributed to the English writer William Penn: "I expect to pass through life but once. If, therefore, there be any kindness I can show, or any good thing I can do to any fellow-being, let me do it now, and not defer or neglect it, as I shall not pass this way again." Next to the quote was a note in DeMarsh's characteristic scrawl: "This I shall endeavor to do."

As DeMarsh unfolded and read this note, he was feeding what psychologists call the moral imagination, a kind of wellspring from which selfless action flows. To kindle your own imagination, think about people you consider "moral exemplars"—those whose outlook and actions you admire. William Penn was an exemplar for DeMarsh; others might include historical figures like Rosa Parks, influential teachers, or family members. By finding and returning to such exemplars, you grow more willing to help those in need. You create the conditions for brief candles to ignite—and for a well-paced, fulfilling life.

Absorbing the Light

Another way to orient yourself toward brief candles is to soak in their light as they happen. Rick Hanson, who studies how experience shapes the brain, has developed a strategy he calls "taking in the good": thinking about brief, enriching moments in ways that help you create more of them.

Our minds have a natural tendency to focus on negative events, Hanson says, mostly because doing so can be a good survival strategy. Ancestral humans who scanned the horizon for threats—a band of rivals, a Bengal tiger—may have been more apt to pass their genes along, but this so-called negativity bias often has little value in the present. Focusing on the positive aspects of emotionally fraught or significant moments is one way to correct the mind's negativity bias, enabling you to learn from your successes, as well as your mistakes. "The playing field is tilted against us," Hanson says, "so we've got to level it."

When you light a brief candle, you can take in the good by savoring the positive emotions you experience in these moments—an approach akin to sipping a glass of wine rather than bolting it down. Reflect on your sense of joy and contribution, paying attention to your physical sensations, as well as your emotions and subjective impressions. This kind of multimodal experiencing, as Hanson calls it, engages areas of the brain's cortex that are involved in memory formation, etching the moment more deeply into your mind.

As you grow accustomed to taking in the good, you'll strengthen the brain pathways that help you to do so. Feeling joyful and excited after a brief-candle experience can trigger the release of a brain chemical called norepinephrine, which in turn prompts new brain-cell connections to form. Over time, your brain becomes more receptive to encounters you consistently find fulfilling. You'll grow more inclined to approach challenging but rewarding situations, Hanson says, rather than avoiding them. "You really can change the settings inside your own brain over time."

These neurological changes help explain why reflecting on brief candles can motivate you to look for more of them. One day in 2004, Luma Mufleh made a wrong turn on her way home and wound up in the parking lot of an apartment complex near Atlanta, Georgia. There, she spotted a group of refugee kids playing soccer. She felt an impulse to join them; in her hometown of Amman, Jordan, people had often entered pickup games on a whim. "I had a soccer ball. The boys wanted it," she remembers. "We had rocks set up as goals." Focusing her attention on the kids, Mufleh felt an instant flare of connection with them, since they were facing many of the same challenges she faced when she first arrived in the United States.

As Mufleh drove through the neighborhood that day, she was overwhelmed by the scent of wisteria, a flowering vine her grandmother had grown back in Jordan. "She had taken me to my first refugee camp at the age of eight," Mufleh says. "I got very emotional." As she reflected on her pivotal experience with the kids—taking in the good, as Hanson would put it—her sensory impressions of the day brought back memories of her own refugee childhood and of those who had cared for her during those years.

Fresh off these joyful, multilayered impressions, Mufleh decided to join the kids' soccer game again on another day—and another, and another. As she learned more about the challenges they were facing at school, she grew ever more determined to turn her full attention to creating opportunities for young refugees. She went on to create a nonprofit called Fugees Family, which now runs a sixth- to twelfth-grade school in Atlanta that serves more than one hundred refugee students. If not for Mufleh's reflections the day of that first parking lot brief candle, which ignited so many others, her larger mission might not have come to be.

Passing the Flame

When priming and attention work in concert, as they have for Luma Mufleh, the result can be a kind of virtuous cycle. Focused, deliberate attention fuels joy and fulfillment, and those inner returns prime you to light still more brief candles, igniting another round of connection and contribution. The deep sense of purpose that grows out of this cycle sustains people like Mufleh and Stange through fast-paced, difficult days—and has helped them thrive in ways independent of what they earn or accomplish.

Since the brief-candle ethos doesn't rest on external returns, the inner rewards that fuel the cycle may be the only assured ones. Joe DeMarsh, however, was fortunate enough to find out what happened to the student he'd shown mercy to decades before. As George Ting reflected on the impact DeMarsh had on his life, he realized he wanted to thank his old principal in person. With help from staffers at his alma mater in Japan, he managed to locate DeMarsh, who was then living in Pendleton, Oregon.

By the time the two men got back in touch, DeMarsh was more than ninety years old and suffering from kidney failure. Ting arrived at DeMarsh's bedside in Pendleton just in time to remind DeMarsh of the brief candle he'd offered Ting so many years ago—and to thank DeMarsh for his forgiveness in Ting's most vulnerable moment. Two days after their talk, Joe DeMarsh passed away.

Kurt Stange, too, has witnessed the uncanny persistence of long-ago brief candles. When he cultivates a basic foundation of trust, conversations that last less than ten minutes can nonetheless extend people's lives and allow them to flourish for months or years. There's the disgruntled employee he talked out of brandishing a gun at work, but there's also the older woman who caught her colon cancer early because Stange had advised testing after noting she looked paler than usual. And there's the longtime smoker who decided to quit after pivotal office chats—and with Stange's encouragement, followed through.

These brief candles, all of which were ignited in ordinary moments, helped create worlds that wouldn't otherwise have existed. It's this alchemy that has kept Stange flourishing through a demanding career, generating returns he never foresaw. "When you start paying attention, it gives you a sense of abundance," he says. While millions believe, with near-evangelist fervor, that grunt work gives rise to abundance, Stange, Mufleh, and DeMarsh have found a less arduous route to it: catapulting someone else into the rest of their life.

Chapter 9

Selfless Pacing

Ever since **Abby Reyes** hiked Utah's majestic Escalante River Canyon, flanked by undulant slabs of red rock grazing the sky, her life had revolved around one goal: protecting the environment from those who sought to destroy it. After graduation, Reyes began working as a legal advocate, helping Indigenous people protect their land from petroleum companies seeking to extract its resources for profit.

Reyes's journey took a tragic turn when Colombian rebels killed Terence Unity Freitas, her boyfriend and fellow activist, and left his body in a field. Freitas had worked with the Indigenous U'wa people to defend their land from resource extraction. In the wake of his death, Reyes redoubled her commitment to environmental justice. She knew there was more work than ever to be done: more letters to be written to lawmakers, more radio interviews to tell the world what the U'wa were facing.

"People's lives were on the line still, and the protection of that land and those waters were in the balance," she says. "I just kept going."

Eventually, the stress of pushing her limits began to show up as physical symptoms: back pain and joint misalignment so severe she had trouble getting around. "I had to relearn how to walk," she says. Though Reyes knew intellectually that she needed to conserve her health and energy, she wasn't sure how to do that without feeling she was betraying the cause.

Reyes had run up against the unique pacing challenges that accompany a range of selfless ventures, from activism to nonprofit leadership and caregiving for dependent family members. Too often, the tasks and causes that galvanize you can also ensnare you, compelling you to offer up your time and energy well past any reasonable limit, and scuttling your ability to serve others in the long run. Staving off this outcome requires what psychologist Abraham Maslow called a "healthy selfishness," safeguarding your own energy and welfare so you can commit to what helps you and others flourish.

"We must be able to go at more sustainable paces," rabbi Danya Ruttenberg writes. "We must build the world we want now—building in care, not replicating the model of exploitation and running ourselves dry."

Giving Until It Hurts

Overstepping your giving limits is tempting because there are so many incentives—both social and biological—to keep going until it hurts. Studies of brain activity during giving support a theory as old as Charles Darwin: Humans are fundamentally wired to want to help others, which is one reason dedication to a cause bigger than yourself feels so rewarding.

Giving engages the brain's mesolimbic reward system in ways that prompt surges of dopamine, the same brain chemical that floods in when you have sex, snort cocaine, or eat a sumptuous meal. Allan Luks, former director of Fordham University's Center for Nonprofit Leadership, has documented the euphoric "helper's high" devoted altruists enjoy, which spurs them to deeper commitment.

Research also shows that dedicated givers are healthier and go on to lead longer lives. In one study, volunteers had healthier blood pressure and blood glucose levels than other participants, putting them at lower risk of conditions like heart disease and diabetes. In another study, people who volunteered one hundred hours or more per year proved less likely to die over a four-year period than non-volunteers. Activism offers similar benefits: It often confers a sense of belonging that's tied to better physical and mental health. In general, when you stake part of your identity on service—whether you're a dedicated volunteer or a caregiver—you're better poised for long-term flourishing.

But the positive reinforcement you get from helping can also pull you in so strongly that any notion of balance goes by the wayside. It's easy to get addicted to the rewarding dopamine bursts you get when you contribute. Almost without realizing it, some pathological givers start to chase these dopamine bursts, sacrificing their health and well-being in the process.

What's more, when your identity is anchored in contributing to your community or loved ones, it can feel disloyal, if not immoral, to pull back. It's one thing to demand that your unreasonable boss pay your promised overtime wages. It's quite another to back off from heading up a donation drive, knowing that if you do, dozens of deserving children might miss out on holiday gifts.

People who are highly attuned to others' feelings may be more vulnerable to giving too much. "They really have an innate desire to make other people happy," says engineering professor Barbara Oakley, an editor of *Pathological Altruism*, a book of essays about the perils of overgenerosity. The desire to make others happy can make givers feel highly distressed at the prospect of throttling their pace, Oakley adds. "Your own empathy can get you to do things you shouldn't be doing."

This empathy-fueled overcommitment is common among family caregivers, the majority of whom are women. "I have little time to myself to handle personal chores, to simply relax and unwind at the end of the day," one woman caring for her father posted in a support forum. "Lately, I've found it so hard to be positive and provide my best care. . . . I feel so guilty and selfish admitting these things, especially knowing how much my dad still struggles on the daily."

After grappling with her own helping exhaustion for a long time, Abby Reyes knew she needed a deeper kind of renewal, so she moved to a teaching center near Santa Cruz, California, to focus on her yoga practice. But even there, she felt so strongly about the causes she was working for that she was unable to stop risking her well-being to support them.

"I learned how to breathe. I learned how to sit with myself," she says. "I also convinced them to give me a cabin, not just for where I was living, but a second cabin so I could run all this political work." Though she was grateful for her expanding mindfulness practice, she still often felt as if she were in a race against time—one she needed to win.

The communities to which givers belong sometimes make the problem worse without meaning to, encouraging greater and greater levels of sacrifice. These communities often have an entrenched "culture of selflessness," which sounds like a good thing but can actually mean members urge each other to unhealthy extremes. At many nonprofits, it's par for the course to put in overtime without much of a pay bump. Similarly, more than 40 percent of people who provide unpaid care for family members say they rarely or never feel relaxed, and more than 50 percent say caregiving takes a toll on their mental health. Under social pressure to embrace their roles, moms and other caregivers often feel like they're not doing enough, adding to their psychological burden.

The hustle ethos of "always on, never enough" can get just as entrenched in community and family groups as at Fortune 500 companies. Sometimes it gets even more entrenched, because contributors believe so strongly in the value of what they're doing. The irony is that in trying to right the wrongs harmful systems inflict—human rights violations, inadequate healthcare or childcare—givers can end up perpetuating the unhealthy pace at which those systems run.

Part of the problem, says researcher and Equity Literacy Institute founder Paul Gorski, is that the same dogged qualities that fuel engagement in helping ventures can lead people to ostracize those they think aren't committed enough. In one environmental organization Gorski studied, a certain leader became infamous for chasing away other key contributors. She sometimes worked as many as twenty hours a day, and she shamed others whom she saw as less dedicated.

Under this kind of pressure, people who just want to help community members or loved ones end up driving themselves to chronic exhaustion. While an over-giving ethos may be the norm in some community or family groups, it's not an ethos that can be sustained. "It's one that churns through people," Gorski says, "and just hopes there are other people we can plug in."

The Sisyphus Dilemma

Activists and volunteers often start out on fire, deeply involved in their altruistic work. But relentless pressure to overcommit wears down their enthusiasm, breeding apathy and disengagement that can persist for weeks, months, or even longer.

At this point, helpers start to show familiar physical signs of unaddressed pacing problems, says human rights scholar Cher Weixia Chen of George Mason University. Their blood pressure may go through the roof. Their mood may plummet. They have trouble focusing on anything for more than a few minutes. They feel estranged from the very people they're trying to help—and they have trouble pacing themselves in other aspects of their lives as well.

"I was really, really, really depressed," one of Chen's interviewees, Bethany, told her. "And I said, I have to do something about this, because I didn't even have energy to play with my children."

The struggle only compounds when dogged efforts to drive change don't have the anticipated results. You may spend years mentoring a young student, only to watch her family and loved ones talk her out of pursuing a degree program she's dreamed of. You may spend weekends lobbying against a bill that's making its way through Congress, only to watch the bill pass the new legislative majority that's just been swept into power. Or you may spend hours each day supporting a family member through a mental health crisis, only to watch them continue to struggle.

This kind of mismatch between effort and results takes its own distinct psychological toll. If you're caught in this bind, you may feel like Sisyphus of Greek myth, who repeatedly rolled a boulder up a hill only to watch it roll back down. But while Sisyphus had to keep pushing up the boulder for eternity, helpers and activists may become less motivated each time the boulder rolls down, and they often contemplate quitting.

In one revealing study, people made an earnest effort to serve the greater good—in this case, by putting trash into different bins for recycling. But afterward, some were told that their efforts had been for nothing, because an assistant had dumped all the bins together into the same trash bag. People felt deflated when they learned what had happened, and many said they'd be less likely to go to the trouble of helping the environment next time around. In situations like this, "You wonder, *Is it really working? Does it really matter that I do all this?*" Bethany told researcher Chen.

As a result, some givers retreat into apathy, figuring that they might as well not engage at all. "The initial fire of enthusiasm, dedication, and commitment to the cause has 'burned out,'" psychologist Christina Maslach and her colleague Mary Gomes write, "leaving behind the smoldering embers of exhaustion, cynicism, and ineffectiveness."

When longtime helpers burn out or quit, their departure has profound ripple effects on the communities to which they belong. For every lifer who leaves a nonprofit group, for instance, the group loses years or even decades' worth of practical knowledge—and that brain drain makes mentoring other members more of a struggle, Chen says. "It's detrimental to the change we hope to achieve."

Practicing Healthy Selfishness

It's natural, and often necessary, to take time off from helping once you've reached full-fledged burnout. At the same time, permanent withdrawal comes with its own downsides. When you leave, you lose the psychological benefits that stem from making real contributions within a giving community—offering a mentee or ill relative much-needed encouragement, or hosting events that support a cause and bring people closer together.

Yet by veering closer to the middle of the pacing spectrum, you can still reap these benefits while forestalling potential harms. When psychologist Abraham Maslow studied groups of what he called "self-actualizing" people—those who'd mastered the art of putting their talents to best use—he noticed that they had often negotiated such a balance. "We find in our subjects a healthy selfishness," he wrote, observing that they showed great respect for themselves as well as others.

More recent research underscores the rewards of healthy selfishness and how it contributes to smart pacing in service work. Columbia University psychologist Scott Barry Kaufman reports that people who score highly on a "pathological altruism" scale—meaning they identify with statements like, "I have little time to myself because I am so busy helping everyone"—are more likely to suffer from depression.

However, those who score well on a "healthy selfishness" scale—identifying with statements like, "Even though I give a lot to others, I know when to recharge"—have higher levels of fulfillment and a true desire to help others with no strings attached. Those two attributes are integral to sustained service and to sustained flourishing. It's easy to assume that discontent with the current state of things is what inspires us to do selfless work, but Georgetown University's Kostadin Kushlev and his team found that happy people are *more* likely to take action to help the planet than are their less happy counterparts.

When chronic back and hip pain forced Abby Reyes to take the rest she'd put off for years, she started to reckon with the impossible pace she'd been keeping. Powerless to unclench the frozen muscles around her spine, she burned to resume her work. Yet her collapse drove home a truth she'd been resisting: To go on contributing for years to come, she'd have to put her physical and mental health first, no matter how seemingly endless the work in front of her. "The river is not going to change. The river is accelerating," she says. "To be of any service at all, I have to figure out how to be a whole human being while in the slipstream."

One way to define your own version of healthy selfishness is to think about what specific tasks you're most prepared to tackle and which ones others may be better equipped for. If you're a gifted writer and communicator, you might enjoy (and excel at) promoting upcoming events online but bow out of attending budget meetings or spearheading donation drives. If you have a family member with health challenges, you might volunteer to prepare meals for them but decline housecleaning and toileting duties.

Thoughtful streamlining proved crucial for Abby Reyes as she recalibrated her pace. "It was important for me to locate myself on the spectrum so that I could see where I was contributing and understand that other people in the ecosystem were playing these other roles," she says. "That was a huge relief to me. It quieted the noise of overwhelm."

In her early teaching years, Barbara Oakley went out of her way to help her students tackle any academic issue, minor or major. But once she realized her above-and-beyond approach was sapping her energy, she thought about how she might ratchet down her involvement while still supporting students. When she started asking her students to approach other class members for help before they contacted her, the tide of requests began to recede, and she had more energy to help students with truly urgent needs.

Taking more time to mull over potential giving commitments can also help you set a healthier selfless pace. Oakley points out that we often make decisions about service based on what psychologist Daniel Kahneman called "fast thinking"—snap judgments based on simplistic ideas about generosity ("helping makes you a good person," for instance). Once we make those snap judgments, they tend to crystallize in our minds as "right responses," leading us to cherry-pick data that support them.

To reassert balance, try orienting yourself toward Kahneman's "slow thinking" approach. Evaluate how well a service commitment fits with the rest of your life and explore how you actually feel about it. Beyond the help you can provide, how much do you enjoy this particular activity—whether it's mentoring, advocating for those in trouble, or sharing food with those in need? How meaningful are the contributions you can make in this role? Reflecting on questions like these can help you decide whether or not to maintain a commitment. "If I'm a little bit resentful, I can tell, 'Well, that's a no,'" Oakley says. "It works out pretty well."

As you decide, your own mental limits should remain at the forefront. Your colleague might thrive on teaching middle school workshops gratis several days a week, but if you're an introvert, that pace might leave you feeling more burned out than energized.

After Abby Reyes clarified what kind of helping work she most enjoyed—outreach, curriculum planning, and connecting people—she decided to focus more on those areas while leaving other logistical tasks to trusted colleagues. Since making this shift, she's found that not only does she have more time to rest and recharge, the time she spends at work feels joyful and even restorative.

Like Diane Allen, the concert violinist who thrives on "getting into the music," Reyes now achieves a flow state when she takes on meaningful tasks at which she excels. "The learning edge for me right now is feeling restful while engaging," she says. Throughout the day, she offsets these stretches of focused engagement with breaks, knowing from experience that if she tries to blaze through without stopping, the mounting physical and mental consequences will undermine her ability to contribute.

Flourishing Within Giving Communities

It's crucial to seek out and foster support groups that reinforce your attempts to find a saner giving pace, helping you find joy and positivity amid the inevitable frustration of service work.

In response to waves of burnout, some nonprofits and community groups now offer members and employees yoga training, meditation classes, and other self-care perks. However, these programs may not achieve their full potential without organizational changes that help people set healthier rhythms. The problem isn't the lack of self-care resources, Equity Literacy Institute founder Paul Gorski says. "The problem is the absence of the *community* care."

Group members can set the tone for this communal care in how they respond to those who approach them with pacing concerns. If someone says they have to step back or take a few days off, supporting that move helps establish a group ethos that allows people to attend to their needs, rather than denying them until their inner reserves dry up.

At the University of California, Irvine, Reyes now leads a program designed to help threatened communities build resilience to climate change. When she brings leaders and community members together to discuss goals, Reyes engages the whole group in what she calls "strategic questioning," a practice she learned from activist Fran Peavey. During this process, people can share openly about obstacles they've faced, giving them a chance to offer meaningful support to one another. This foundation of mutual support helps them address open-ended questions that sharpen the group's shared objectives: What would you most like to see happen? What specific action can we take to get closer to that goal? What kind of backup do you need?

These kinds of clarifying questions make it easier to figure out what well-defined role each member of the group can play, so that no one feels overwhelmed or overextended. They encourage a flexible, responsive group ethos, which helps make giving and caregiving feel manageable and fulfilling rather than onerous.

Many committed helpers "go straight from 'Everything sucks' to 'I have to act,'" Reyes says. "We neglect these strategic middle pauses of, 'Yeah, everything sucks. Well, what *do* we want it to look like? What would need to change to get there?'"

While volunteers and activists may find opportunities for these fruitful exchanges within the organizations they serve, caregivers often face more challenges in building supportive communities. Some have few extended family members living nearby, while others feel isolated from relatives who are less involved in hands-on care. In such cases, joining local networks of other caregivers—such as Caring Village, Las Madres, or Family Caregiver Alliance—may be the best way to find solidarity and set a more measured pace. Others who understand what you're going through can help you pause and negotiate different ways forward when you feel depleted and overwhelmed.

Sustainable giving communities also find ways to recognize contributors as more than their assigned tasks, rejecting pressures to define them in terms of their productivity or the roles they fulfill.

Paul Gorski has been involved with several organizations that negotiate this pacing challenge well. In one education-justice panel he took part in, "at the beginning of each session, we would just chat: What are you passionate about these days? What are you working on outside of work?" Gorski says. He appreciated participants' efforts to get to know everyone in the group. "They're modeling that it's okay to have whole other parts of your life, and it's okay to renew ourselves through connecting." Extended families, too, can take a cue from this approach, checking in to connect with primary caregivers on a regular basis.

Celebrating milestones also helps selfless communities build long-term viability. It may be true that the work is never really done. But by building in deliberate, joyful pauses—a night out to mark a nonprofit's tenth anniversary, a banquet for volunteers who mentor hundreds of young students each year, a celebratory family dinner—groups can highlight the human impact of people's contributions, energizing them in ways that keep them engaged.

"How do you build community around being perpetually disaffected? There's got to be some pivot to joy," Gorski says. "It's the most sustainable way."

Staying in the Game

Finding celebration and joy in intense helping work can demand the patience of a marathon runner and then some. You have to accept the way progress surges forward and sideways and then seems to double back on itself—much like hero's journey narratives that vacillate between triumph and despair.

Every long-term quest includes victories: a major grant or account secured, an ailing relative healed, a rally that starts a groundswell of public involvement. But those victories are often infrequent, sandwiched between long stretches when not much is happening or when past progress steadily erodes.

Since real-world change often proceeds in punctuated equilibrium, focusing on the selfless efforts you're making—which are themselves tied to life satisfaction—is a surer route to steady flourishing than banking on a certain outcome that may not materialize for a decade, if at all. "We have successfully been conditioned by capitalism and the attention economy to expect rapid results," writes activist Dylan Keese-Forster. "We need to conserve our energy so we can stay in the race."

Like other approaches that set your life's overall tempo, pacing in the service realm demands a complex mix of stubbornness and fluidity. While Abby Reyes has always been stubbornly devoted to the work that matters most to her, she's come to realize that fluidity in daily matters—a willingness to take a few days off to tend to her health or to delegate essential tasks to someone else—is precisely what keeps her core commitments intact. As a young activist, she felt she didn't have the luxury of that fluidity, given the scope of the problems at hand. "There was an illusion that I didn't have agency," she says, which kept her logging superhuman hours that destroyed her health.

Asserting agency can feel uncomfortable at first, especially for activists and helpers who came of age when self-sacrifice was the cultural norm. But there are signs, experts say, that this norm is shifting considerably.

When Chen started her research years ago, "there was a dominant culture of martyrdom," she says. But in recent months, more organizations have reached out to her wanting to learn about how to build lasting giving communities. "It's very gratifying, even though this change is gradual—from a culture of martyrdom to this emerging concept of a culture of health."

The altruist's credo has always been that by making others whole, you make yourself whole—and it's true that service to others, pursued at a reasonable pace, helps you thrive physically and mentally. But by renouncing cultures of martyrdom, Reyes, Chen, and thousands of others contend that you need to make yourself whole before you can sustain the wider world.

Chapter 10

Dropping off the Map

t's the last weekend of July, and the line of cars outside Paris's Gare de Lyon train station is lengthening by the minute. Though I'm less than a half mile away, the line of glowing red taillights in the tunnel extends as far as I can see, and horn blasts echo off the tiled walls. My cabdriver's GPS says the station is still sixteen minutes away. Passengers are jumping out of nearby cars right and left, and I can't blame them. Walking seems like a much better bet.

This is the *chassé-croisé* (crossover), one of the busiest travel weekends of the year, and a cultural event in itself. It springs from a unique intersection in time: French people who've been on paid vacation for the whole month of July, termed the *juilletistes*, are returning from extended breaks, the so-called *congé annuel*, in the French countryside or elsewhere in Europe. The same weekend, an even larger group—the *aoutiens*, who will be on vacation most or all of August—set out for their own destinations.

Once I reach the jam-packed station, I scan for a forgotten corner where I can sit on my suitcase. The Gare de Lyon's halls often throng with business travelers, but today it's almost all families, older people, and children. Everyone's dressed for summer holidays—shorts, sundresses, high-heeled espadrilles. Tiny dogs sit at their owners' feet, surrounded by a welter of duffels, fast-food bags, and backpacking gear. The human traffic moves in pulses: The hall empties as trains board for southern France or Italy, then swiftly fills again with new arrivals.

As France's train stations become hives of nonstop activity, its population centers turn into temporary ghost towns. Across Paris and other French cities, signs saying *Fermé*—Closed—hang in shop doors for much of August, especially at family-owned businesses. While larger museums remain open, many smaller ones shut down, and restaurants shutter by the dozens. It's a clear signal of just how seriously people take their breaks. "Vacation in France," sociologist Jean Viard of Paris's Sciences Po university told a reporter, "has taken the place of the great religious rites."

From a pacing perspective, alternating focused work periods with extended time off makes practical sense. Athletes have always had off-seasons that allow them to buffer mental and physical stress, while in traditional farming cultures, families move into seasons of rest once the crops come in and the days grow shorter.

More recent research shows how longer breaks renew depleted physical and mental reserves in ways shorter ones simply can't. At best, bite-size workday breaks "are restorative," says University of Washington management researcher Kira Schabram, "but they're never transformative."

Extended breaks, those lasting a few weeks or longer, are a different animal. The freedom they offer can prompt big-picture reassessments and insights that permanently shift your course. They also facilitate smart pacing in both the short and long term. As they replenish physical and mental reserves that have been drawn down by months or years of overwork, they equip you to make career and life changes that sustain you over the course of years or even decades.

"The days were like great sunny plains," diarist Etty Hillesum wrote of her idyllic time in the Dutch countryside, "each one a long, uninterrupted whole." The vast sunny plain of the extended break is fertile ground for transformative change, clearing the way to long-term flourishing.

Since fewer than 20 percent of US companies offer paid or unpaid long breaks, temporary withdrawal on this side of the Atlantic can feel like a subversive act—the equivalent of escaping to Walden Pond. But with some advance planning, designing an extended break is more feasible than it seems—and it may be the pacing shift with the most power to direct your future steps.

A Lesson from the French: You Are Not Your Job

Nearly a hundred years ago, France's *congé annuel* tradition began as a reaction to excesses in the other direction. Most French workers in the early twentieth century spent well over half their waking hours on the job, an established though grim fact of life. But things began to shift after left-wing Popular Front groups took power in 1936, promising French voters "bread, peace and liberty." To that end, representatives passed new laws requiring employers to give workers at least two weeks of paid vacation each year.

The cultural movement the laws sparked took on its own momentum. At the height of midsummer, family sedans roamed the country, crammed with tents and towels and umbrellas. Campgrounds sprang up, eager to cater to vacationers, and workers returned from long breaks glowing, their energy and motivation restored.

This collective enthusiasm gave rise to laws that not only maintained free time allotments but also extended them. By the 1960s, the paid August vacation was as much a French stalwart as foie gras or the "Marseillaise" anthem. Today, French workers are legally entitled to at least thirty days of paid annual vacation, translating to about five workweeks, as well as a separate allotment of holiday leave.

The French commitment to extended rest goes well beyond the letter of the law, says Michael Mendolia, the CEO of French firm Business Crescendo. Not only do people stay away from work during midsummer breaks but they also try their level best not to think about work at all, fending off invaders who try to get into their headspace.

Before people leave for vacations in France, Mendolia says, they often create auto-reply messages that announce they won't respond to incoming emails any time soon. "I've even heard of a case where someone said it will be automatically deleted," says Mendolia, who grew up in the United States and has lived in France for over a decade. (The French government is all in favor of such boundaries, enacting legislation like the "Right to Disconnect" law that states employees don't have to reply to work messages during time off.) The cultural zest for disconnection is so ingrained that if, for some reason, you opt out of the *congé annuel*, you might even get side-eyed. "If you tell people you're not going on a summer break," says my French friend Katie Callan, "they look at you like, *Why not?*"

French attitudes toward vacation and retreat reflect a broader belief that work should remain at the periphery of a well-lived life, never approaching the center. In many circles, it's considered déclassé to make any job your identity. It's not normal to ask people what they do right away, Mendolia tells me. Instead, people are more likely to talk about subjects like their political views, what they've been reading—or, yes, where they recently headed on vacation.

Listening to Mendolia, I think about just how much Americans rely on the question "What do you do?" at parties and gatherings: at once an icebreaker, an attempted show of interest, and a means of establishing the social pecking order. I've never considered these aims when I use the line myself, driving it home with follow-ups: "How did you get interested in that?" "What projects are you working on?" But the French disdain for such questions underscores how they reveal what we value—and, by omission, what we don't.

The Restorative Power of Long Breaks

Versions of the French attitude toward rest and retreat flourish in distinct pockets around the world, at schools and workplaces where people take regular long breaks. Such breaks—now called sabbaticals in academic and some corporate circles—actually originated centuries ago among manual workers. Much as ancient peoples took the Sabbath as a rest day after working the remainder of the week, farmers often took a year to let fields rest after six years of intensive harvests.

As the Industrial Revolution unfolded, some knowledge workers started taking up the sabbatical cause, having learned that the breaks helped them stay energetic and even-keeled during busy stretches of their careers. It wasn't long before the concept became ingrained in academia. In 1880, Harvard started giving professors a year off after seven years of work, and by the 1930s, more than 150 universities boasted their own sabbatical policies, offering faculty periodic yearlong breaks for travel or independent study. "During my thirteen years as president," William R. Ross, head of Colorado State College, wrote in 1961, "this policy has been of infinite value both to the individual teacher and to the college."

In some ways, the rise of the modern academic sabbatical paralleled the rise of the French-style extended break. At first, small groups of specialists demanded longer stretches of time away from work. But once the breaks took root—in legislation or in official university policies—people raved about their benefits, triggering a broader cultural shift that cemented the sacrosanct status of those breaks.

These shifts preceded much in-depth analysis of what people actually gained from their time away. Only in more recent years have researchers analyzed the full impact of extended breaks, how much restorative potential they offer, and how they affect people's mood and energy levels.

In one study, Tel Aviv University researchers compared the well-being of 129 faculty members on sabbatical to that of 129 others who stayed on the job. As expected, the stress levels of the sabbatical takers dipped below their initial baseline, both during and after the break, and their life satisfaction rose after they took time off. But the most intriguing finding was that the life satisfaction of the control participants *decreased* over the course of the study. That suggested people on sabbatical had steered clear of a dip in mood they might have suffered if they had remained at work.

Later, researchers at the Netherlands' Radboud University studied vacationers who took breaks of a little longer than three weeks, on average—the near equivalent of the *congé annuel*. Once people's vacations began, the team found, their health and life-satisfaction levels didn't peak until the eighth day they'd been away, strongly hinting that breaks should be longer than a week to maximize their restorative power.

While some of these vacationers enjoyed adventurous activities like hiking, those who spent their time relaxing logged their own strong improvements in health and mood during their breaks. That suggests that the activities you choose during your break are less important than simply disconnecting and spending your days the way you want. Break-takers' sense of control over their time off, in fact, predicts how contented they will feel afterward. When you cram your days off with frenzied activities you think you *should* do—thus bringing overachiever energy into an extended break—your time away can rapidly become more draining than restorative.

Though the US work world has been slow to acknowledge the lasting benefits of extended breaks, a few outlier firms have been talking them up for years. The software designer firm Autodesk gives its employees six full weeks off after they've been with the company for four years, while Silicon Valley's Intel Corporation offers workers eight weeks off for every seven years of work. Like their counterparts abroad and in academia, employees report that these breaks not only restore their depleted energy reserves but also reset their work pace and reorient their priorities.

When former Intel employee Benzi Schreiber embarked on his extended break, "I went down my contact list and noted how many people I'd lost contact with over the years," he wrote on social media. Before his break, Schreiber had worried about losing his job, but when he caught up in person with old friends, those work worries receded because he was having such a blast connecting with people he loved. "When a job goes away, they are still there for me. I now nurture them and cherish them the way that I should have done decades ago." Like many French people, Schreiber had come to see work as one peripheral element of life, rather than as the linchpin around which everything else revolved.

Career Resets

In the town of Valensole, off France's well-beaten tourist path, the mental din of email pings and to-do alerts recedes. Set on a Provençal plateau high above the country's southern coast, Valensole's cobblestone landscape feels plucked from another century. The scent of lavender hangs heavy; flowers in the surrounding fields have just been cut for the year, soon to be processed into soap and sachets and essential oils. In ancient caves carved out of stone walls, locals browse jars of organic honey.

Just off the main street is the home of French communications specialist Carole Schaal, who has found renewal in Valensole for more than twenty years. When she was younger and short of money to buy a Parisian flat, she stumbled upon the town and fell in love with a stucco house on a gentle slope, flanked by a multistory vine of red trumpet flowers. The price was right and the timing was perfect. "I was looking for something of a nest," she says. "It was very important for grounding me, because I had moved so much."

Securing such a retreat was always top priority for Schaal. Born and raised after the Popular Front's ascendance, she's taken *congés annuels* her whole life. These days, she returns to Valensole in August with her teenage son; it's a golden month with little planned besides grabbing market lunches and hanging out laundry in the sun.

As we sit in Schaal's light-filled living room, she explains that she can't get into full vacation mode right away. "It takes a while to change pace," she says. "I need at least a day or two—to rest from the traveling and let go of the tensions. And then I still need a little bit of time to stop checking my emails."

Schaal's need to ease into disconnection aligns with the research showing that energy and life-satisfaction levels peak only on the eighth day of vacation—and it also jibes with my own experience. On weeklong vacations, I so often want to do nothing at all but read and relax. I sometimes feel guilty that I don't want to do something more active with my family: kayaking, biking, surfing. But Schaal's perspective confirms that what looks like sloth on the surface can be a necessary prelude to recovery.

When Schaal is more than a week into the *congé annuel*, she says, a distinct transition starts to happen, one that illustrates why the break matters so much. Once she's shaken off work doldrums, she settles into contemplating larger questions: What does she most want to contribute? What fresh direction does she want to strike out in? "New ideas come," she says. "Not only new ideas, but memories, stuff that you forgot about."

It's those ideas, she continues, that allow her to get clearer about where she is now and where she wants to head next. For her, this introspective process has become essential. If you, too, seek out such a contemplative period, you can use it to reflect further on the goals and values that Ben Rogers's re-storying prompts from chapter 3 may have brought to the surface. "You need to have a clear picture of the whole situation," Schaal says. "You need to make a conscious choice of where you want to be."

Such reflective periods in Valensole have helped guide some of Schaal's most important career transitions. She took a position as communications director at an environmental nonprofit after taking time to reflect and recharge. That sustained reflection helped her realize she wanted to contribute more actively to energy-efficient building projects in France.

"Do you see a relationship between the time you take to renew yourself and your ability to have that higher vision?" I ask Schaal.

"Big time," she replies.

That theme resurfaces later on, when I head out for drinks with Laure Gaillard, who works for Marseille's city government. Like Schaal, Gaillard has taken *congés annuels* nearly her whole life; when she doesn't take these breaks, she notices that her energy levels tank. But the longest work break she took, she says, was the most impactful. Tiring of the daily grind of her desk job, she signed up for a yearlong stint doing organic farming in places around the world. In classic French fashion, her employer assured her that her job would be waiting when she came back.

The trip, though hardly relaxing in a standard sense, was exactly the reset Gaillard needed. "I learned about myself, about my capability in dealing with any situation," she says. When she lived with farmers in rural Washington state, soaking up their love of the land and dedication to sustainable growing, she felt hooked on it and fulfilled in a way she never had before. "I realized, in America, this is my home," she recalls.

That realization bent the arc of her career. After returning from her travels, she launched into a new role: her region's chief of staff for sustainable food initiatives. She now educates businesses and consumers about organic farming's importance and how to implement it broadly—one of the most ambitious programs in France. For both Schaal and Gaillard, *congés annuels* haven't just supplied necessary time to recharge; these built-in breaks have also launched them onto new, fulfilling career paths where they continue to flourish.

Designing Your Extended Break:
How, When, and Why

The renewal Schaal, Gaillard, and many others enjoy on their long breaks—the kind that ends up directing their future steps—has become an obsession for the University of Washington's Kira Schabram. Early in her career, Schabram worked at nonprofits, where she saw spectacularly high rates of burnout, as people kept grinding on no matter how depleted they felt. Once she moved to academia, she resolved to find practical ways to stave off this outcome. "Coming from the nonprofit world where there's never enough resources," she says, "I'm always interested in interventions that any organization could do."

Schabram started zeroing in on the potential of extended breaks when she met the entrepreneurship scholar DJ DiDonna. DiDonna had become an evangelist for long breaks after taking one himself. He was looking for academic colleagues who could help explain the surprising perspective shift he'd experienced during his own time off. To figure out what explained the restorative power of extended breaks, Schabram, DiDonna, and their colleagues conducted in-depth interviews with fifty people in their twenties, thirties, or forties who had taken different kinds of long breaks.

People in the study had all sorts of reasons for going on break. Some took time off to finish a specific passion project, some sought a life reset through quests like hiking the Appalachian trail, and others were simply so burned out they could no longer go through the motions at work. In general, you should think about taking a long break whenever you start feeling—like some of the group's interviewees—that you're heading toward a cliff, physically or mentally. As a preemptive measure that helps you return to equilibrium, it makes far more sense than trying to regroup after a full-blown crash.

Almost without exception, study participants reported that their time away spurred positive changes in their careers and lives. At the beginning of their time away, many interviewees focused on recovery activities—say, doing yoga or spending more time in nature—for weeks on end. Their data support previous research showing that, up to a point, the longer your break, the more replenished you'll feel at the end. While a monthlong break like the *congé annuel* certainly promotes more recovery than a weeklong one, Schabram and DiDonna say that for maximum recovery benefits, at least six months are ideal. And while US workers often hesitate to take long breaks because that goes against the corporate grain, employers were often curious about what workers had gained during their time off; some said they wished they could take their own long break. In fact, some interviewees reported being the center of attention (and the object of envy) among friends and colleagues when they returned from their breaks.

If you're looking to make a major change in your work life, a "questing" extended break—one where you expose yourself to new ideas and approaches, rather than committing to a specific project—may be the best choice. These more open-ended breaks, Schabram found, were more likely to touch off major life and career metamorphoses. "It's like having a whiteboard that's completely clean," one of Schabram's interviewees told her. "We get to figure out how we want to fill that space." Detailed break planning, which might seem like a sensible idea, tends to clutter the frictionless plane that encourages fresh ideas and approaches.

Looking back, Alysia Gonzales wishes she'd realized this from the outset. After Gonzales started a one-year break from her job as a technical writer, her first instinct was to catch up on all the chores and social obligations she'd set aside over the years. "I was, like, 'Oh my God, this free time is finite. I need to take advantage of it,'" Gonzales says.

A few weeks in—amid an endless sequence of friends' birthday parties, closet-cleaning stints, and meetings with home contractors—Gonzales felt more drained than she had when she was working full time. Her long break, meant to be a refuge, had become another attempt to prove her productivity to herself and the rest of the world. Taking extended time for contemplation went against the grain because it didn't involve making measurable progress toward a pre-set goal.

It was only when Gonzales cleared her mental decks, giving herself open-ended time to think, that she started making headway on the fiction writing that had prompted her to take time off. As her long break went on, she gradually shed the inner aversion to idleness that had defined her for many years—something she wouldn't have been able to pull off on a shorter break. She also recognized how cultivating her own version of the open, frictionless plane enriched her output and helped her flourish creatively.

"You're not just sitting and watching paint dry on a wall. Or even if you are doing that, there are still things your brain is doing that are crucial to forming deep, complex thoughts," she says. She recommends that would-be long breakers allow themselves one to three months of very few expectations. "It was necessary for me to ask myself, 'What happens if I become a slug?' and be able to do that and have the world not collapse."

Free-Range Extended Breaks on a Budget

Clearing your own open plane can give you the time and mental space to strike out in fresh directions. But if, like most Americans, you don't have a supportive boss or copious savings to draw from, you may conclude you'll never be able to clear that kind of space. Traditionally, sustained breaks have been privileges inaccessible to many of us, especially small-business owners or employees who have few days off or guaranteed benefits.

In the United States, we conspicuously lack the social infrastructure that has democratized pace slowdowns in places like France. But even without this kind of social support, you can design an extended break of your own, without a huge nest egg or an employer's blessing—provided you plan strategically enough in advance.

As Vanessa Gray toiled at her job in the healthcare sector while managing her deceased parents' estate, she realized she could no longer maintain the work and life pace she'd been keeping, doing what amounted to a second, volunteer gig on top of her paid one. "I said, 'You know what? For me to get my head on my shoulders and stop reacting to problems, I'm going to need to take a break.'"

With trepidation, Gray quit her full-time job and embarked on a self-imposed six-month break. Her savings account was hardly flush, so she knew she'd have to cut way back on expenses to make things work. As she drew up a strict budget, she reached out to family members who offered some modest support to get her through her six-month leave.

Even with these assists, Gray couldn't completely quell her anxiety about making ends meet. But once her extended break started, she realized how much she had needed this uncluttered stretch of time to orient herself. "I gave real thought to what I wanted the rest of my life to look like," she says, "asking myself where I wanted to go and what I wanted in five years or ten years. Every day, I was giving myself an assignment of sorts, to start really pondering those questions."

In the early weeks of her break, Gray got more involved in her community, attending local classes, taking workshops, and spending time at the library. Through that exploration, she began to realize she wanted to be more involved in creating and sustaining the kind of strong community she'd come to appreciate. As she researched her career options, she found out the government was hiring planners to design thriving communities at military sites around the world.

Gray decided to take a government job in urban planning after her break wound down. Without the deeper reflection she did during her sabbatical, she says, she might never have moved into a specialty that suits her so well—which made all the planning, saving, and belt-tightening worthwhile.

To design an extended break like Gray's on a limited budget, consider precisely how you're going to support yourself and your family during the break, whether that means saving up a few months' worth of money for expenses or reaching out to friends, family members, or mentors who might be willing to help fund your mission. "If you set up the circumstances," Gray says, "the ability to take a chance like that is available to you."

In addition, if you want to resume your current job when your break ends, you can try lobbying your employer for support (financial or moral), making a case that your leave is in their best interests, as well as yours. Some bosses fear that once workers go on a long break, they'll skip out for good. But because such breaks help stave off burnout, offering them to employees can actually be a shrewd move for companies taking the long view.

Schabram and her colleagues found that people who took "working holiday" extended breaks, during which they tackled specific passion projects amid stretches of rest and contemplation, mostly returned to their jobs afterward—and they did so with renewed vigor and commitment to their work, balanced by their awareness of the value of retreat. "They're not only going to come back," Schabram says, "they're going to come back refreshed, and they often are very eager to apply what they learned."

The Great Sunny Plain

The more I learn about the shifts and realignments that arise from long breaks, the more curious I've become about what it's like to take them regularly. Unlike Carole Schaal, Vanessa Gray, and Alysia Gonzales, I have little direct experience with what I'm missing. Deep rest is like a rare creature I've read about but never seen close up.

As my time in Valensole winds down, I ask Schaal for her advice on how to approach an extended break. "Take it as a project of taking care of you," she says slowly. "Define what it is you need in your mind, in your body, and allow yourself to do something new. Don't rush into the decision. Just think about the questions that you've never asked yourself."

I think of how Laure Gaillard opted to take that crucial year off from her job, and how that decision likely sprang from her strong sense—honed through decades of *congés annuels*—that the break would give her the freedom to ask herself questions she hadn't asked before, as well as the mental bandwidth to pursue the answers. It's an acquired skill: stepping out onto a plateau you can't yet see, trusting that the ground will be there to support you.

The biggest advantage of carving out your own *congé annuel* isn't that it will renew you for months on end. It's not even that you will reconnect with friends and family in ways that help you keep work in perspective. It's that—whether for a few weeks, a few months, or a year—you will rise above the static of daily life to reach Etty Hillesum's great sunny plain, the uninterrupted whole in which something of the numinous, the unexpected, or the sublime can take up residence. And as retreats launch you in new, surprising directions, you come to appreciate how self-defeating it is to zoom along on a single course without pause.

Watching vacationers funnel through the Gare de Lyon station, toting their suitcases and scarfing down their pastries, it's easy to lose sight of what's set to emerge after the chaos evaporates. It's no small thing for a population to set out in unison, each person in search of their own great sunny plain.

In the United States and other countries, following that lead, whether by taking long breaks or giving others permission to do so, feels riskier. But the audacity of choosing an extended leave carries over to choices made in the aftermath. The courage it takes to pull back the throttle can help you set a long-term pace that's reasonable for you, rather than caving to an employer's demands. "It made it okay for me to be able to take chances," Vanessa Gray reflects now on her extended break, several years later. "It also influenced people around me, making it okay for others to take whatever types of chances they want." That kind of groundswell effect could ultimately propel a bold collective investment in long-term flourishing.

Chapter 11

Collective Pacing

It's nearly 9:00 a.m., and the conference room on the second floor of Rhode Island Hospital is starting to fill. Brown Medical School surgical residents in slate-blue scrubs chat in small groups, swigging from water bottles and scanning their phones for new pings.

A few minutes after the hour, psychotherapist and performance coach Daryl Appleton—one of the only ones not dressed in scrubs—approaches the front of the room. "Today we're going to talk about developing and assessing trust," she says.

"How many of you are with the people in this room more than you are your own families and loved ones?" One by one, hands go up. Appleton stresses that if they can't depend on each other in the lurch, their work lives are going to descend into a chaos spiral. "Building trust, giving this to your people, is wildly important; you're going to have people that *want* to work with you and for you. This is going to save you time, energy, and mental space to do your jobs."

With her straight talk and early morning ebullience, Appleton exudes lead-anchor charm. In practice, though, she's more activist than affable mouthpiece. Her goal is nothing short of subversive—to disrupt medicine's entrenched, unforgiving rhythms. To that end, she's spearheading one of the biggest reforms in Brown Medical School history: guiding surgeons-in-training to approach their work, and each other, in ways that foster well-paced, decades-long careers rather than five-year flameouts.

Impossible workloads, of course, are older than Methuselah. What's new is supervisors' and CEOs' increasing willingness to renegotiate those rhythms within work teams. In fields like medicine, finance, transportation, and law, employees know sixty-plus-hour workweeks often come with the territory. What they have less and less patience for are unreasonable demands from on high, like being on call at all hours and baked-in cultures of speed that don't respect their physical and mental limits. "Even if I have the best boundaries in the world," says compassion scholar and consultant Leah Weiss, author of *How We Work*, "how can I pace myself reasonably if my team undermines that?"

What makes for a sustainable team pace isn't just how many hours people work—or don't work. An atmosphere of mutual trust and honesty also matters, as does what kind of support you can expect when you're reaching your limits. Groups where members check in frequently with each other, both receiving help and giving it to others, make better decisions on the whole, and their members also report better psychological health. What's more, enhanced team rapport can help stave off individual pacing problems before they manifest. The better teams function as a unit—thanks to supportive atmospheres where people respond to what others need—the less burnout those members suffer.

Collective pacing is its own distinct art, one that can seem impossibly complex. It demands sensitivity to changes in the environment, such as workers' evolving life circumstances, management changes, and fluctuating workloads. It requires assessing how individuals' needs intersect or clash with an employer's broader vision and approach. And it resists simplistic time-based fixes, since cutting people's hours doesn't resolve the kinds of group dynamics that lead to burnout. There's a reason few consultants specialize in this art, at least so far: It can feel like trying to corral a spreading oil spill.

As employers face the realities of thinning ranks, however, they're beginning to engage experts to help them foster empathy, responsiveness, and better pacing within teams navigating intense daily demands. Like surgeons charged with improving patient survival rates, Daryl Appleton, Leah Weiss, and other consultants are upending dysfunctional team dynamics in organizations of all types, gauging how well each new approach works and adjusting as needed. Their approaches are grounded in ongoing input and feedback from each team member, a rebuke to classic management practices of setting the pace from the top down.

A Culture of Trust

Reforming work culture is more feasible these days because employees aren't the only ones calling for a sustainable work pace. Those at the top of the hierarchy are also buying in, spooked by visions of a skilled workforce making for the exits. That exodus began during the pandemic, when more and more workers—under inhuman pressure to do their jobs with dwindling resources—started quitting in droves.

Facing what felt like a free fall, many employers responded with a host of attempted quick fixes. Companies rolled out hour-long yoga classes, massage therapy, and a smorgasbord of wellness and mental hygiene tips. But it soon became clear these approaches were akin to putting a Band-Aid on a gaping wound. Amid horrendous workplace conditions, half an hour of downward dog seemed like a bad joke. "If I have to listen to one more 'eat well, sleep well, do yoga' conversation, I'm going to throw up," one emergency medicine doctor told me during the pandemic. It's become clearer than ever that individual wellness counseling, no matter how well intended, can't heal entrenched collective dysfunction.

Paring back work hours isn't the answer on its own, either. When people think about pacing themselves on the job, they might consider shifting a seventy-five-hour week to a fifty-hour one, or sandwiching longer breaks between extended work stints. But as consultants like Appleton note, group-level pacing isn't just about how many hours you put in. It's also about what happens during those hours—whether team members feel like they're being heard when they raise concerns, and whether they're given the resources and time they need to do their jobs.

If you're embedded in a team where you're expected to churn out peak performance with very little support, no workload is going to feel manageable, whether it's thirty hours a week or eighty. And under these conditions, as companies are starting to recognize, employees' output tanks. As levels of "toxic workplace" traits like rudeness and cliquishness increase, according to a Shanghai University study, workplace productivity plummets.

While managers want to avoid such outcomes, Appleton says, many of them simply don't understand how to foster collective flourishing. "They do the 'Let's get together and let's have doughnuts and coffee,' but it doesn't actually help." A 2019 Harvard study, in fact, showed that most work wellness interventions did not measurably boost employees' general health, and had little effect on their job performance or mental health.

Daryl Appleton's program offers an alternative to the Band-Aid approach, fostering pace changes on a more structural level. Brown's surgical department commissioned her to head the program in the interest of setting up its residents for sustainable long-term careers—something the medical profession hasn't always done in the past. "No one teaches you, 'How do I pace?' Sometimes they find themselves not knowing the answer," Appleton says. "For the first time, we're actually starting to teach it, live it, and have language around it."

Throughout the academic year, Appleton meets with groups of residents—newly minted MDs still completing their practical training—and attending physicians who supervise those residents. Meeting topics range from how to cultivate trust in tight-knit work groups to how to have hard conversations with difficult people, the kinds of "soft skills" long de-emphasized in medicine.

To supplement these regular meetings, Brown Medical School has kept Appleton on call for more than a hundred open-ended hours each year, much of which she turns into one-on-one meetings with surgical trainees and young doctors. "I see everything from 'I have to have a hard conversation. How do I word this email?' to 'I don't know how to task prioritize' or 'I miss my family.' We work on action-oriented steps like 'What's the obstacle? What's the fix? What do you need to do next?'"

The surgical residents Appleton advises work up to eighty hours a week, and their jobs are inescapably demanding. Given these priors, Appleton leans into the idea that what makes for a sustainable work pace isn't just how many hours you log (or don't) but also how many social shock absorbers are built into the system. The level of give-and-take you can expect within your team. How people treat you when you disclose mental health struggles. How well your supervisor listens when you tell her you don't have the resources to do your job—and whether she follows up with a solution.

Among the most crucial of these shock absorbers, Appleton stresses, is an atmosphere of mutual trust, since most teams can't function effectively without it. In one of her seminars, Appleton asks the residents how they decide whether someone is trustworthy. One by one, they venture answers: You know they have a strong track record; you know they have the right training to respond to the situation. Then the discussion turns to what happens when you *don't* trust the people you're working with.

One resident says he gets wary when he has to jump into a trauma case partway through and no one else is clearly explaining what has happened. "I get scared when I don't hear anything, because then it makes me wonder, *What the hell's going on?* Now I have to start checking, doing *their* job," he says. "Having the interns who communicate and say, 'Hey, this seems a little weird,' or 'Hey, I'm not sure about this'—that allows me to trust them."

The objective, as in Appleton's other seminars, is to foster a team atmosphere where everyone feels supported and is able to air what's on their mind. That kind of mutual trust, says Ken Lynch, the Brown residency program's director of surgical education, goes a long way toward helping people maintain a pace that feels comfortable and sustainable. If they know they'll be listened to when they speak up, they stand a much better chance of solving energy-draining issues that arise.

Lynch urges trainees to approach him and Appleton for help long before they reach burnout's bleeding edge—because he cares about them, but also because he knows that residents who hit a wall may not rejoin the program for months or years, if they ever do. When a resident in their second or third or fourth year exits surgery altogether (or, worse, quits years past certification), the training and knowledge they accrued over the years is lost. That imposes more pressure on the doctors who remain, putting them, too, at risk of burning out.

Appleton's work is meant to be a check against this doom spiral, and so far, the results look promising. While in the past many trainees clammed up within their work teams, afraid they might be branded as weak if they were struggling, a shared ethos of disclosure is taking hold. No matter what's going on in the residents' lives—family problems, conflict with old-school supervisors—Appleton reminds them that they don't have to shoulder it alone. "We have a resource for it," she says. "You don't need to continue to fail forward."

Putting Everything on the Table

In a light-filled backyard office unit in Portland, Oregon, Leah Weiss has assembled her own blueprint for team pacing. A compassion and workplace expert trained in Buddhist meditation, Weiss consults with companies around the country, helping them build work teams where members feel supported and energized enough to make meaningful contributions over time.

For companies keen on documenting results, one of Weiss's strengths is her focus on gathering objective data. When she starts working with small teams, she likes to do baseline assessments of how well these teams function. Then, after teaching them strategies for engaging in constructive, thoughtful group dialogues, she'll do another assessment weeks or months down the line to see if their functioning and team dynamics have improved.

Weiss sees her approach as a potent means to a larger end: promoting equity and group problem-solving in a world where hierarchies and top-down orders dominate. From a young age, Weiss, the descendant of Holocaust survivors, couldn't resist pushing back on unjust school rules. "I definitely inherited this 'If you're not fighting against what's wrong, then you're part of the problem' kind of ethos." Her spiritual grounding, too, started early. As a teen, she meditated, read the *Tibetan Book of Living and Dying*, and absorbed her teachers' messages about the importance of compassion and community.

At one early, career-defining job—as an education lead at Stanford University's Center for Compassion and Altruism Research and Education (CCARE)—Weiss straddled the practical and the transcendent, incorporating brain-science findings into community classes on mindfulness and compassion.

At first, Weiss focused on teaching re-centering practices that people could try themselves, like meditation. But she soon saw the limits of this individualized approach. She could teach clients to meditate at companies and in community settings, and they could start a regular practice, but if they felt like their work environment was impossible or their bosses shut down their concerns, they'd still be miserable and burned out.

As the years went by, Weiss also began to grasp how profoundly the go-it-alone approach had failed her. As she juggled work and raising three young children, difficult coworkers often brushed aside her pleas for flexibility. Despite her regular meditation practice, she soon felt utterly burned out and started overeating to smother her frustration.

She recognized, too, that it wasn't just her. In so many organizations she'd worked with on mindfulness initiatives, something seemed rotten at the group or cultural level—and her suspicions were confirmed as she explored further. When she combed through surveys and interviews from outgoing employees at different companies, she realized that about three-quarters of respondents were leaving their jobs because of problems related to their manager or team. "If there's culture work happening, the individual isn't enough," she says. "Very few people are addressing the team level."

Given these issues, Weiss decided to focus more on advising small-scale work groups, which she had realized were conveniently nimble. Organizations could spend millions of dollars trying to teach thousands of employees some leadership or communication skills, but without near-universal buy-in, that entire investment could vaporize.

On the other hand, a single supervisor adopting collaborative team principles could make life far easier for the five or ten people reporting to him or her, even if upper management stayed stuck in its rigid ways. When Weiss works with one small team within a larger company, she's found that leaders are more invested in her programming, since there's no top-down attendance mandate involved. Instead, "it's the manager saying, 'I want to do this,'" explains Weiss, and that genuine commitment helps generate similar buy-in from team members.

At the beginning of her work with clients, Weiss often asks members of each four- to sixteen-person work team to take a survey to gauge their current levels of burnout and resilience. The survey takes personality factors into account, such as anxious tendencies, and specific job requirements that are especially stressful. At the end of this process, each team receives a report that highlights the risk factors for burnout within the team, as well as any protective factors. (Though each person's individual score is confidential by default, people can choose to share their scores with other team members.) The goal is to make sure each member has a basic understanding of strengths, weaknesses, and preferences within the team.

After this baseline is set, teams hold regular meetings to ensure each member feels supported. These meetings often begin with each person checking in about how they're doing, then they zero in on specific pressures the members are facing. If one team member is overwhelmed by new projects that keep being piled on, for instance, the whole group will discuss how to moderate that workload—and how to implement a pace change that doesn't adversely affect other team members.

As team members learn to be more forthright and flexible, they reach "a place where they can have the hard conversations, like, 'It drives me nuts when I'm about to go on vacation and you plop this down on my desk,'" Weiss says. "You can't just make the decision to change your cadence of work on your own. It actually is a team-level problem." Over time, team negotiations start to become more forward-looking as members almost reflexively ask others if they need support—a practice that can help stave off pacing meltdowns altogether. This dynamic recalls a striking proposition from evolutionary biology: Cohesive and supportive social groups often thrive better over time than internally contentious ones.

Shifting away from the stoic, go-it-alone approach, however, is rarely easy or straightforward, Weiss says. When team members' goals conflict, the teams have to hash out whether a fair compromise is possible—and, if not, whose view should carry the day. And when those views clash, deep-rooted issues may arise without warning. A colleague's dismissive comment about maternity leave, say, may confirm a working mother's gut sense that she isn't being taken seriously—and potentially remind her of past instances when someone with more seniority brushed her needs aside.

Resolving issues like this with nuance and empathy helps cement team trust. "The thing that's really interesting about the team level is you're blending together some things that are super pragmatic and some things that are subtle emotional wounds," Weiss says. "It's all mixed together in one big soup."

The Proof Is in the Pudding

Stylistically, Daryl Appleton's and Leah Weiss's approaches to functional team pacing diverge. Where Weiss has designed planned activities and surveys to assess team progress, Appleton's approach revolves more around providing team support on demand. Yet both programs aim to set the same kind of cultural baseline, establishing open expression, discussion, and adjustment as group norms that solidify over time.

The crucial question—especially given the dollar and time investment employers are making—is how well these programs manage to build teams where members establish a culture of trust and support each other in setting a workable pace. Though most studies so far have been done in-house, there are signs these cultural interventions are starting to deliver. At companies that have signed on for Weiss's program, cases of severe burnout dropped by 47 percent over a three-month period, and about 70 percent of employees noticed positive changes in their teams within the first two weeks. And while studies of Appleton's program are still underway, initial data show burnout rates dropping among residents who are enrolled. Brown officials say concepts like how to prioritize duties and how to manage difficult moments come up much more in conversations within teams.

"Our residents today are more open about that stuff. And I think they're able to balance these stressors better," says Ken Lynch, who tries to model this forthright communication with the young doctors he oversees. In the culture Brown is working to create, Lynch says, the message is, "Come talk to me, let's have a discussion. You are not supposed to be perfect. We all are here to learn."

Other team pacing trials have also shown promising results, including one that consultants ran with a forty-person team at accounting firm Ernst & Young. Facilitators from the Energy Project had each employee commit to pacing practices, such as taking a short break for every ninety minutes worked, and when employees shared concerns about their workload in small, trusted groups, other team members pitched in to help them tackle those issues. Following the team's busiest season, team members reported feeling better and more energetic than they had at the same time the year before. They also bounced back more quickly from fatigue, and they seldom quit their jobs—more than 95 percent of employees stayed on board.

Installing New Pacing Cultures

For teams and workers invested in setting a healthier collective pace, the first challenge is often getting buy-in from bosses. Leah Weiss once had an exchange with a CEO who seemed interested in improving her work teams' dynamics but backed off when she realized how much effort and investment it would require. "On paper, she saw all the limitations of meditation and yoga-based strategies. But then it gets real, and you're asking this person, 'Are you really going to address the changes that come up in the data?'" Weiss says. "The honest truth is, a lot of leaders want to do it until they don't want to do it."

Still, she says, overstretched workers have plenty of options even if upper management shies away from broader pacing resets. Managers of individual work teams can implement regular team check-ins, encouraging members to speak frankly about the challenges they are facing and offer support to others. Such sessions can evolve into something akin to Fran Peavey's practice of "strategic questioning," in which team members grow accustomed to asking each other what they need and what actions they can take to get closer to their shared goals. These meetings need not drag on; just ten to twenty minutes every week or two, Weiss says, can help members feel more comfortable and supported in their roles.

At the end of each meeting, the teams can come up with an action plan to address functional challenges. If, for example, some team members have a habit of interrupting or downplaying other members' struggles, the group can ask them to commit to holding their peace long enough for others to finish speaking. To help members follow through on commitments they've made, managers can lead a discussion in the next meeting about how much progress the team has made toward its goals.

One way to foster such supportive environments, says Valor Performance founder Sarah Milby, is to hire trained consultants to counsel team managers and supervisors first (either one-on-one or in a group), teaching them how to foster strong workplace relationships by encouraging open, respectful dialogue. Such one-on-one interventions, Linköping University economist Lina Koppel and her colleagues have found, sometimes "spill over" and create broader cultural changes. "As a manager or a leader, how you're approaching certain conversations, issues, and processes is going to have a ripple effect on your team," Milby says. If managers make a habit of asking team members how they're managing their workloads and offering backup when things get hairy, team members may soon start doing the same with one another.

Workers' relationships with direct supervisors are among the most crucial in any organization, Leah Weiss points out. When people bail out, it's often due to a manager's impossible expectations, and when they stick around for the duration, it's because they feel valued for what they bring to the team and are comfortable raising concerns, pacing related or otherwise. Among the more successful groups she's advised, she says, are those headed by managers who don't want team members' jobs to feel onerous. These bosses understand that fostering a sustainable team pace is in everyone's best interest.

Resetting the Balance

In the long run, collective-pacing advocates view their work as a critical kind of social repair. They seek out this work for the constructive friction it generates—the way it tips people toward necessary engagement and away from ennui. Weiss is very conscious of investing her effort where she's likely to see the most payoff. On the most impactful projects she's worked on, "there's superstrong internal championing," she says. "When there's turnover and shrinking resources, it's pretty impossible."

But even limited corporate investments in team pacing can have a knock-on effect, provided the right people are involved. After Sarah Milby helps organizational leaders handle their own work-pacing challenges, those leaders grow more skilled at responding to struggling employees. Daryl Appleton has noticed a similar evolution, strengthening her belief that collective-pacing shifts can have generational impact. Once senior residents reject the idea of running junior employees into the ground—the way their own superiors did—the junior employees may emulate those new norms when they go on to mentor the next cohort of young doctors.

Such shifting dynamics have inspired Appleton to pitch her approach to other leadership teams around the country. Between impossible scheduling demands and escalating levels of burnout, Appleton says, some level of collective-pacing reform has become almost nonnegotiable. "It's no longer, 'That's so nice. That would be great,'" she says. "It's 'We need to change something.'" While those changes can be fraught and complex, teams that work through them have an inner robustness they didn't have before. Once the cultural balance has been reset toward health and contribution, those who work against it have less power to be chaos agents. Each strengthened member, as in a Roman arch, helps keep the others standing.

Chapter 12

The New Pacing Movement

On a sunny spring day in downtown Atlanta, a little-used church sanctuary stages a reimagined kind of service. Every pew has been cleared to make way for a haphazard tiling of yoga mats, pillows, and water bottles. About a dozen attendees lie on the mats in fetal position; others are prone, facing the vaulted ceiling. Silhouetted against one stained glass window is a bassist in workout gear, strumming pencil-thick strings to conjure a melody you can feel and hear all at once.

The leader of this unconventional service is Tricia Hersey, a theologian and performing artist who's made promoting rest her mission. In addition to hosting nap-ins at the former Georgia Avenue Presbyterian Church, which she calls the "Rest Temple," she travels around the country urging overextended fellow travelers to take time for ease and renewal. She hosted a rest-themed book group at NYU in Manhattan, and in Seattle she helped lead an outdoor "collective daydreaming" event to the resonant hum of sound bowls.

Hersey is among the standard-bearers of a pacing movement that's proceeded in fits and starts through the years but is rapidly gaining momentum. The speed and complexity of modern life have long been established givens. But part of what fuels the movement now is a disconnect between the stillness that reigned during the global pandemic shutdowns and the frantic daily rhythms that have since resumed. Activists like

Hersey and Slow Movement founder Carl Honoré are making the case for leaning into the fleeting stillness we once knew, establishing new, deliberate rhythms that create space for that stillness to expand.

"We've just been told from the time we were little, 'This is the way it is,'" Hersey said at a recent event, urging people to question the unflagging American devotion to work. "Let's begin to uncover and discover, 'Is that really true, and are there other ways?'"

What elevates this new pacing movement beyond self-care cheerleading is its potential to seed the kind of reflection that allows for meaningful response to broader challenges. Deliberate retreat, as Jenny Odell notes in *How to Do Nothing*, is a necessary precursor to confronting such challenges.

"We know that we live in times that demand complex thoughts and conversations," Odell writes, "and those, in turn, demand the very time and space that is nowhere to be found."

The pacing movement sometimes anchors itself in physical spaces: in churches and community centers like the Rest Temple, and in the European "Slow Cities" Carl Honoré has inspired. But much of its momentum also gathers online, on pages like Hersey's Instagram—where her posts have received more than half a million views and likes—or in the comments section of Honoré's inaugural TED Talk, which has more than three million views. Hashtags like #SlowMovement and #StopRestPace attract scrollers trying to reconcile their lives' hard-and-fast demands with their own need to refuel. Online and in person, activists are giving people permission to rest and withdraw in ways that once would have seemed radical.

Though bumper sticker phrases and hashtags like #SlowMovement might seem tailor-made to trend, pacing advocates aren't seeking to establish a one-size-fits-all mantra. On the contrary, shrewd pacing, as Honoré sees it, "could be fast, it could be slow. It could be a marathon, it could be a sprint, it could be anything in between," he says. "It's choosing what musicians call the *tempo giusto*—the right pace for the moment." Advocates like Honoré and Hersey don't just tell people to slow down. They also help people get comfortable traversing the in-between stretches of the pacing spectrum.

But helping people find the right pace can be a complex, contradictory business. Pacing promoters must use the tools of a speed-obsessed society to help people find the *tempo giusto*. To be heard, they must post and plug frequently, crafting messages that generate enough buzz and momentum to trend. And they must hope that people primed to scroll for the next reward will adopt pace-setting as a lifelong project, with all the uncertainty and soul-searching that implies.

Citizen Pacers

While public conversations about pacing have surged over the past few years, many of them sound like riffs on a centuries-old theme. In holing up at a cabin on the shores of Walden Pond, writer Henry David Thoreau staked out his own position against what had already become a culture of overexertion. "It is nothing but work, work, work," he wrote of mid-1800s US society. "I think that there is nothing, not even crime, more opposed to poetry, to philosophy, ay, to life itself, than this incessant business."

Around the country and the world, a growing chorus of people have continued to refine their own versions of Thoreau's refrain. The Italian activist Carlo Petrini—alarmed by the number of McDonald's franchises popping up as late-twentieth-century globalization took hold—has launched what he calls the Slow Food movement, which touts the benefits of local farming, locally grown produce, and unhurried meals shared with family.

At the start of the new millennium, Carl Honoré—then a journalist ricocheting around the globe—took up Petrini's baton. While in a line at

Rome's Fiumicino Airport, Honoré started skimming a newspaper, and a headline jumped out at him: "The One-Minute Bedtime Story." Weary of what seemed like endless story sessions with his young son, Honoré was so intrigued by the article's featured expert and his uber-efficient sixty-second bedtime routine, that he immediately calculated how soon Amazon could send him the expert's entire book collection. But as the line snaked toward the gate, another, opposing thought occurred to him: "Have I gone completely insane?"

That thought propelled Honoré into an overhaul of his fast-paced lifestyle—one he summarized in his first book, *In Praise of Slowness*, released in 2004. In the years that followed, Honoré built a distinctive movement of his own, one that followed Slow Food's lead but broadened its scope to "slow living." His viral TED Talk on the topic cemented his status as a global advocate for dialing back.

As public interest turned toward rethinking uber-efficiency—and as job demands showed few signs of diminishing—other activists began offering their own cases against inhumane work rhythms. When Tricia Hersey was an Emory University seminary student, she felt continually overworked and unheard by people in charge, like a cog in a machine she had no say in running. Sensing she was about to burn out, she took up a practice she'd learned from her grandmother: sitting or lying down for fifteen minutes here, or half an hour there, and closing her eyes. These brief rest stints helped restore her energy and her zest to contribute. To illustrate her insight, she planned a performance art piece called *Transfiguration*, in which she read the reflections of slaves who'd endured punishing work, then slept in a bed draped with sheer fabric panels. For Hersey, the simple act of rest embodied resistance to overwork and all the injustices bound up with it.

Near the end of *Transfiguration*, Hersey invited the several dozen people in the audience to nap with her, and many accepted her invitation. Some passed out so completely that Hersey had trouble rousing them even after a couple of hours. When they woke up, a few had tears in their eyes, realizing how long it had been since they had allowed themselves that much time to recharge.

Tricia Hersey had thought her napping performance art would be a one-time event, but so many people started asking when the next one would be that she launched a series of Atlanta nap-ins. These events, she hoped, would offer an accessible means of collective pushback against the grind—and model a practice of daytime rest anyone could continue to explore.

To date, Hersey has organized more than fifty rest events for a variety of audiences. For an Atlanta art installation called *A Resting Place*, she set up a canopy bed with windblown curtains, placed in an area where trains once dropped people off to relax and heal in the local natural hot springs. Recently, she's staged other events around the country to promote her newest book, *We Will Rest! The Art of Escape*.

As Hersey unveiled her nap installations, the UK-born art director Jo Hawkes was going through her own rest-related epiphany in Amsterdam. When she was a fledgling artist, Hawkes had tackled an arresting assignment: designing a new edition of Charles Dickens's classic *Great Expectations* with larger spaces between the lines of text, a change she hoped would help readers ingest the book more slowly.

Though Hawkes's book design won her a typography contest, other projects soon commanded her attention, halting her plans to publish the work more widely. Years later, during a holiday break, she picked up Honoré's *In Praise of Slowness* and got energized about thoughtful pacing all over again. In spare moments, she experimented with creating her own brand, called PACE Moments. "I had this idea that it could be some sort of a platform that encouraged people to find a balance between fast and slow," she says. "It wasn't about, 'Oh, let's all slow down and sit around meditating all day.' The movement was about finding small moments for yourself to take a breather."

Hawkes stashed away her pacing ideas as other obligations consumed her, but years later, a freak biking accident drove the dangers of overwork home to her more viscerally, inspiring her to revive the PACE Moments concept. Running low on sleep, Hawkes spaced out and swerved into a crack in the pavement. "I was actually doing three jobs in one—strategist, copywriter, and creative director. I just got so caught up, so stressed, and I didn't sleep for three nights straight," she says. The accident launched her body over the handlebars and onto the pavement ahead; emergency-room doctors soon confirmed she had broken her leg. "Lying on the hospital bed, I realized, 'Oh my God, I really have been overdoing it.'"

While she healed, Hawkes hatched a plan for taking PACE Moments to the next level. She reached out to Carl Honoré, and the two of them started developing a planned Amsterdam workshop and a line of PACE Moments tote bags. She launched a PACE website and several social media channels. She hosted "slow morning" sessions, online *kaffeeklatsches* where people would swap ideas about living at a healthy tempo. And she released a series of pacing-themed art prints to remind people they didn't need to perpetually slog. In her unscheduled moments, she dabbled in a slow-paced hobby—planting seeds in small cups and watching, day by day, as the green sprouts poked up through the soil.

The Great COVID-19 Awakening

By the time the COVID-19 virus began ricocheting around the globe, Jo Hawkes, Tricia Hersey, and Carl Honoré had all committed full tilt to helping people establish a more livable pace. They grieved the tsunami of chaos and loss that followed the pandemic's surge. But as the months crept by, the uniqueness of this moment started to register. For some workers on the front lines, in hospitals and retail stores, the pandemic continued to impose demands that stretched them well past their energetic limits. But others—unable to work or working from home on lockdown—found themselves careening into a once-in-a-century stretch of enforced rest. Stressful commutes vanished, meetings were pared back owing to video-chat fatigue, and schedules grew steadily more flexible. For some people, Honoré noticed, that unexpected stretch of rest supplied a counterpoint to their harried former lives.

"If you're living in roadrunner mode and suddenly you're forced to stop, an awkward transition hits. It hurts," Honoré says. "But because the pandemic lasted long enough, people broke through the discomfort. They looked back and thought, 'I was living on autopilot before. I was racing through my life instead of living it. I'm not going back to that.'"

When the lockdowns ended and people began settling back into the grooves of their previous routines, another related phenomenon emerged: nostalgia for what had proved to be a fleeting period of stillness. "I kind of miss the early part of the pandemic," a friend confessed to me. "It sounds terrible." In those first lockdown days, she'd been able to work from home almost every day, which gave her more time to decompress and to bond with her kids. But she was already back to four days a week in the office, with just one work-from-home day for balance.

All over the world, workers are looking to recapture that transient stillness. In China—long known for its twelve-hour work shifts—the *tang ping,* or "lie flat," movement has emerged into the spotlight, urging adherents to reject overbearing work demands. "Even though it looks like I'm doing nothing for six months, I am working hard on myself," worker Crystal Guo told a reporter, explaining why she'd left her job. "*Tang ping* gives me breathing space to reflect on my career and future." And when thirty-five-year-old Bank of America employee Leo Lukenas died of a coronary artery blood clot in 2024, fresh off pulling one-hundred-hour workweeks, fellow junior employees threatened to strike.

Such public statements of intent—continued assertions that the old status quo can no longer hold—have convinced pacing advocates that their mission has a chance to succeed as never before. Honoré saw that views for videos with "slow living" in the title had gone up fourfold within just a year. Meanwhile, Hersey's Instagram account gained about one hundred thousand followers in the pandemic's first year alone, and her follower count has since ballooned to more than five hundred thousand.

Systemic Pacing Barriers

Even as their message gathers momentum, slowness advocates still face the challenge of transforming measured pacing intentions into firm habits. It's not that people dislike the idea of slow eating and slow living, which have been floated before, at different intervals. It's more that they feel the daily realities of their work lives prevent them from embracing those philosophies. Frantic rhythms, however unhealthy, feel natural, ingrained, and inescapable.

Where pacing promoters have been most successful is in establishing a common vocabulary for overwork and in driving home the abstract message that it's bad for you. Most people, including corporate titans, understand it's now taboo to sing the praises of white-hot overcommitment. "When I was your age, I didn't believe in vacations. I didn't believe in weekends," Bill Gates said in a 2023 commencement address, advising graduates to steer clear of his own infamous zeal. "Take a break when you need to. Take it easy on the people around you when they need it."

But it's one thing to recite the gospel of slowing down—or even to sing its praises—and quite another to live it. Even though work-life balance training sessions are now de rigueur for managers, it's still hard to reconcile some pacing stances and rhetoric with the nonnegotiable demands of making a living. A friend of mine recently got an email with a signature that warned recipients they might have to wait for a response because the capitalist ethos wasn't compatible with the life they wanted to live.

On one level, the sender's intent made complete sense (isn't this what we all want, after all—to separate ourselves from the always-on lifestyle that drives stress and burnout?). But we agreed that only someone with a certain level of privilege and security would feel comfortable drawing that kind of line. An assistant manager or emergency-response technician wouldn't be able to mute communication channels at will. Neither would writers like us, deluged as we often are with last-minute inquiries from editors who need to wrap up a piece posthaste.

Though we detest frantic emailing, we also recognize we likely have to do it at least sometimes to keep certain jobs. "It isn't compatible with how I want to live, either," my friend said of the capitalist grind. "But I don't feel like I have a choice."

Workday realities often leave people perched on the edge of deceleration, unable or unwilling to commit to it. Pacing strategies like modulation can offer a gradual way in, allowing reassessment and judicious pullback even when the basic architecture of your workday is fixed. Once Joe Arpaia's resonant-breathing exercises dial down your spun-up nervous system, you can calmly and frankly ask yourself what you actually need (to negotiate a deadline with an over-eager manager? to shut down your email just for a few hours?) and go on to make the next wise choice.

Pacing's PR Problem

What also makes pacing activism such a slog is that so many people see the whole venture as bimodal: either you're living life at a sane, measured pace or you're not. When people encounter pacing movements in their social media feeds, the messages they receive can feel sunny and simplistic, an effect that has more to do with the medium's limitations than with the subject matter itself.

The kind of content that makes the movement trend—hashtags like #StopRestPace, exhortations like "Embrace Rest"—can also make it seem removed from real life. Waves of come-lately "Snail Girl" influencers on TikTok and Instagram, eager to get in on the slowness action without having any real connections to the movement, contribute to the problem. Since these influencers' vibes about pacing are so obviously saccharine, it's hard for followers to take their advice seriously or to implement it in lasting ways. Like million-dollar Bora Bora jaunts, pacing overhauls may be aspirational for many viewers, but they can also seem inaccessible and abstract, easy to gawk at and then scroll past.

As committed advocates point out, though, there's nothing rarefied about true pacing shifts—and they are seldom absolute. Movement leaders talk with depth and nuance about fitting slow moments within the contours of lives that don't permit drastic measures, like quitting your job or telling email senders you won't answer anytime soon because you're sticking it to the man.

At events, people ask Tricia Hersey how to reconcile the "We Will Rest!" ethos with the demands of a nine-to-five job. She'll mention that her inspiration is her grandmother, who worked two jobs, and in the snippets of time between shifts and other obligations, who would sit on the couch with her eyes closed for half an hour. Hersey's message has more to do with clearing space for rest alongside work than with urging people to withdraw from work entirely.

To convince more people to take up the baton, a new strain of slowness messaging highlights the nuance and flexibility at the heart of successful pacing. Advocates of "selective mediocrity," touted by physician and Instagram influencer Whitney Casares, are less focused on telling people to slow down or rest more. Instead, they counsel followers that when onerous tasks arise, from filing taxes to fielding urgent emails, they ought to complete them—but to do so by fulfilling the minimum requirements, an approach Casares describes as "doing something half-a$$ on purpose." Send the two-line email if it answers the questions posed in the three-paragraph one. Race through the project evaluation sheet if you're pretty sure your boss is just going to skim it and toss it aside.

What elevates the selective-mediocrity approach is that it feels realistic in a way that going full Snail Girl or opting out of capitalism doesn't. At its best, mediocrity messaging also conveys a counterintuitive truth: that working too hard, and too indiscriminately, undermines your goal pursuit. Going above and beyond on rote tasks, as psychiatrist Joseph Arpaia notes, is self-sabotage. It drains energy that could be channeled toward more interesting and important goals. "You need to do 'good enough,'" Arpaia says. "But don't do more than good enough, unless you're just absolutely passionate about it."

It's a take roughly in line with Carl Honoré's flexible idea of *tempo giusto*—the right pace for the moment. While pacing will always involve ongoing self-scrutiny, selective mediocrity offers a simple, subversive way to approach the decision-making that shapes daily rhythms. It offers a concrete means to the "We Will Rest" end, no matter which influencers' stars rise or fall.

Achieving *Tempo Giusto*

From Thoreau onward, slowness movements have been urging people to go farther into the wilderness—at least figuratively—to determine what pace might work for them. They don't offer the numbing comforts of mass movements, in which everyone believes or thinks the same way. Instead, they call on adherents to create their own modes of resistance, to reject the entrenched systems that keep the hamster spinning that wheel.

Long-term pacing advocates understand that Snail Girl posts, social feeds, and napping installations are all just potential ways in, doors that open onto a lifetime's work. While the practical impact of the pacing movements has been gradual, what its proponents have started to provide is a collective mental space for figuring out what *tempo giusto* can look like when so many are bent on zooming past it.

In a culture built on Henry Ford's assembly-line ethos—and on education systems that grew out of demand for drone-like workers—pleas for renouncing uber-efficiency are sometimes going to sound like howling into the wind. In addition to keeping current followers' interest amid the daily grind, pacing promoters face the challenge of appealing beyond their base, so to speak: converting millions who have no inclination to check their speed.

Movement-bearers persist, however, because of what they see as the collective stakes. For Honoré, shrewd pacing is about far more than individual flourishing. Global perils, he argues—authoritarianism, runaway climate change—are rooted in the way we choose fast-twitch priorities (comfort, certainty, heedless consumption) over society's long-term health. "There's a real feeling at the moment that everything is about to fall apart," he says, adding that speed drives much of this destruction. "If we keep going down that road, I shudder to think where we end up."

Nonetheless, Honoré remains an optimist. What he foresees, given the rising awareness of speed's perils on multiple levels, is a collective reset period—one where Americans lean into pacing as a lifesaving practice of calculated resistance. "We'll look back twenty years from now," he says, "and think, *Why did we think it was so hard to slow down? Why didn't we do it sooner?*"

It's telling that Honoré bundles a two-decade cushion into even this rosier scenario. He acknowledges that this is no standard advocacy movement—and how could it be, when the threat to be banished resides mostly within? The savviest pacing promoters model withdrawal practices that are flexible enough to weave in, around, and through complex, busy schedules. They grant that much of the structure of modern life is fixed in place, at least for the time being, and they argue for making the most of the interstitial spaces that remain. They remind us to take full advantage of the under-explored middle of the pacing spectrum, whether by practicing modulation, doing daily speed reassessments, trialing solo or group nap-ins, or embracing selective mediocrity.

For Jo Hawkes, a necessary pace reassessment has led her to set aside broader pacing outreach for the time being. Balancing a full-time design job with caring for her school-age daughter has stretched her to her limits, something she's not afraid to acknowledge these days. "We're making it work," she says, "but it means that stuff with PACE has appropriately gone on pause." If, as Carl Honoré predicts, collective demands for saner pacing reach a tipping point—an upsurge of will that takes on its own momentum—the movement will roll on, led by new champions and founding ones who come back restored enough to multiply their impact.

Course Corrections

For years, Michele Benoit set her sights on climbing the marketing world's ranks, and she surpassed her own expectations with flying colors. As corporate clients clamored for her insights, her salary rose along with her expertise. She knew she'd be set for life, at least financially, if she continued on this path.

But as Benoit's life expanded in some ways, it contracted in others. While she enjoyed her work to some extent, she also felt perpetually on a treadmill. Most people logged long office hours at the agencies she worked for, and Benoit feared people might question her dedication to her job if she diverged from the workplace norm. In unscheduled moments, she'd daydream about being able to set her own pace. "Wouldn't it be great to just go out in the middle of the day, have lunch, and go work out?" she remembers thinking. "I want to be that person."

Benoit's first move about a decade ago, after she took a break to do some soul-searching, was to go freelance. The decision felt liberating. She was no longer as beholden to punishing office schedules, which meant she actually had time to do things like exercise and eat lunches in the park during the workweek.

But after a few months, Benoit still felt unsettled. Though she had more control over her work schedule on an hourly basis, she was still grinding, working on uninspiring projects like the ones she'd done before. Though she sensed there might be another, more radical shift in her future, she wasn't yet sure what it might look like.

Pacing might seem to imply steadiness, rhythm, a metronome's reassuring tick. But recalibrating your pace is often anything but a steady process. It's more like letting go of the handlebars and willingly disorienting yourself in the name of reorientation. Though Benoit gained some breathing room when she adjusted her work and break rhythms, she eventually realized that those adjustments on their own weren't enough to help her flourish. She'd hoped her life would snap into focus after her first pacing shift, but the way forward still looked blurry, plunging her into deeper questioning about where she was headed.

Like any engaging narrative, lifelong pacing involves setbacks, unexpected twists, and forays into the unknown. In a very real sense, it's risky to cast off the routines and prescribed goals drummed into us as synonymous with success. But as Benoit came to realize, it can be riskier to hold on to them. Productivity culture idealizes the kind of rigid focus that gives you a sense of control, but ultimately, that rigidity can control you, blocking off other approaches to work and life.

Taken to its zenith, long-term pacing is a flexible, almost playful pursuit, one that makes room for stretches of expansion, contraction, and uncertainty. It's in being willing to flail a bit—to venture into what feels like the belly of the whale—that you'll find the stability you need to flourish.

What gets you closer to thriving, on a daily basis and beyond, are low-key but ingrained habits of self-appraisal. Not self-appraisal in the achieverist sense—fixating on all your failings—but a less loaded kind of appraisal, the kind distance runners do as a matter of course. It involves assessing where you are now, where you want to end up, and what adjustments are apt to get you there.

This might seem like the most basic calculus in the world, and for many endurance athletes it becomes as intuitive as breathing. The difficulty lies in committing to this frank assessment when there are so many incentives to detach from it.

The most deeply rooted of these incentives are social and financial. So many of us are embedded in school, family, and work cultures that encourage self-denial in the pursuit of self-elevation. The default mode is to suppress your desires, and even your needs, to secure some payday or status boost that's just around the corner. When you've been in this mode for years, the distinction between what you're supposed to want and what you actually want is blurred. It's possible, even common, to devote yourself wholeheartedly to a goal, to embrace it and talk it up to others, then acknowledge years later that it's a hermit crab shell you should have cast off long ago.

During periods of slowdown and pause, you can begin to see the hermit crab shell for what it is—an impetus to redefine where you want to end up. Michele Benoit started questioning her own long-held goals during the pandemic lockdown, when she started working from home every day. In her own room, in new, stubbornly unscheduled stretches of time, she contemplated the future in ways she never had when she was following old rhythms. "When you're in your space, there's not a lot of room to hide," she says.

In the midst of this reckoning, Benoit started considering other options. She'd always been a natural helper, mentoring younger colleagues and helping friends talk through their problems. Realizing that the parts of her job she liked best had to do with guiding others through course corrections, she decided to get certified as a career and life coach.

Benoit's daily pacing shift propelled her into a mental space where she could begin to reassess her long-term plans. *Congé annuel*–style retreats offer one kind of entry into this mental space; Ben Rogers's re-storying process, by prompting you to consider your values and potential legacy, offers another. By orienting you toward goals that feel meaningful and away from Potemkin village ones that look grand but ring hollow, these practices instill engaged rhythms that align with flourishing. What helps us thrive in the long run is "not the discharge of tension at any cost," writes Victor Frankl, "but the call of a potential meaning waiting to be fulfilled."

Even so, a deliberately paced life runs just as surely on small, everyday decisions as on necessary, big-picture assessments. Whatever your chosen intention, putting it into practice demands its own granular skill set. It's easy to get bogged down in the minutiae of seemingly mundane pacing choices: *How many meetings will I schedule this week? How long a lunch break will I take today?*

Yet in another sense, your small, daily decisions draw from the same source that fuels the more momentous ones: the kind of ongoing appraisal that clarifies what energizes you, what drains you, and what informs you when you've hit an absolute limit.

When I committed myself to longer-term pacing, after years of shifting between overwork and exhaustion, I had sweeping ideas about what that commitment would look like. I wanted to emulate the way marathoners predicted what was ahead and adjusted their tempo to match it.

It took me months to realize this kind of anticipation wasn't some elaborate chess game. It was natural to think about what obstacles might crop up weeks, months, or years down the line, but that didn't mean I had to fixate on them. On a daily basis, if I felt stressed or overwhelmed and wasn't sure what to do next, it was often enough to follow Amy Baltzell's bare-bones pacing template. First, I'd ease my nervous system into a lower gear, which became more natural when I started practicing modulation. Next, I'd spell out what I needed or wanted to do that day, or over the next few days. Finally, I'd consider, *What's the wise choice here?*

Your biological signals lend an added dimension to this daily appraisal. When you have a hard time deciding how much to double down or pull back, your body's indicators—say, a few days in a row of low heart rate variability or escalating blood pressure readings—become crucial points of reference. When you have evidence you're putting yourself at physical or mental risk, it's easier to justify slowing down or changing course.

Such course changes need not be dramatic to be impactful. Understanding that pacing involves moving along a spectrum, rather than ricocheting between absolutes, multiplies the wise choices available to you. Though your first instinct may be to bail out of a project or commitment, extending the deadline or paring back your hours may be more conducive to long-term flourishing if the commitment matters to you. In the same way, instead of leaping full bore into something new, you can sign on for an hour or two a month, then titrate upward.

This kind of iterative adjustment, grounded in a frank assessment of what you need, often becomes self-reinforcing. As you adjust your pace and tolerance levels, the heedless sprints and snap decisions that were once daily givens start to feel glaring in their wrongness, anomalies that demand correction. And as the pace you've set generates its own rewards—physical and mental resilience, an enlarged sense of contribution—it takes on momentum, becoming more difficult to disrupt.

As their impact accumulates, small, everyday pacing shifts can bend the broader arc of your life in surprising ways. I understood at the outset that practicing modulation each day could help me feel better in the moment, ultimately ratcheting down the anxiety that had been my default state for so long. What I didn't foresee was how it would nudge me toward the kinds of decisions that set me up for longer-term flourishing. In a less activated state, as Joe Arpaia calls it, I'm less apt to heedlessly agree to a work project I have little interest in, one that would have me slogging against my will for weeks at a time, or to make some offhand remark that upends a relationship.

For Michele Benoit, a simple daily pacing shift—revamping her work and break schedule when she went freelance—helped propel her toward reimagining her entire career. The new daily freedom she'd allowed herself gave her space to ask, more directly than she had before, *What's the wise choice here?*

As these shifts shape our individual trajectories, they play into our collective fate as well. Nationally and globally, we are failing to pace ourselves toward finding viable solutions to the climate crisis or viable ways to preserve the earth's resources. We sabotage our future well-being in misguided attempts to preserve the status quo, though so much about it is unworthy of preservation.

These failures are rooted in a rugged ethos of one-upmanship that's proved ferociously sticky in the United States and societies that follow its lead. This ethos stems from other, still deeper-rooted ideas—that the best way to live is to aggrandize the self, and that in order for someone to win, someone else must lose. These entrenched ideas have spawned a succession of social ills: an economic system that prizes growth over long-term sustainability; a political system that rewards shows of dominance and cruelty; an education system that devalues nonlinear thinking; an online universe built to monopolize our attention and deplete our savings rather than enrich our lives.

Faced with counterproductive modes of juicing productivity, it's easy to conclude we're stuck with them for good. Yet if sustainable pacing practices are ever to emerge on a global scale, they must begin on a human one. When you log out of social media for a week, rest under your desk between meetings, or quit your job and give yourself a month to decide what comes next, you create space for others to follow your lead. You model taking time to recover, think, and plan before plunging back into the fray. As self-repair becomes socially contagious, it can also become a catalyst for meaningful collective repair.

In a shortsighted, always-on culture, however, these repair attempts take no small amount of courage. While death-defying heroic acts cluster at one end of the bravery continuum, closer to the middle—and far more accessible—is everyday, necessary stubbornness: a refusal to sacrifice our lives and principles on the altars of productivity, dominance, and self-promotion.

It takes courage to let children grow and explore at their own pace when other parents opt for academic "enrichment" courses billed to supply a competitive edge. It takes courage to quit a high-octane job that makes you miserable when everyone around you is toasting to your success. It takes courage to stand behind your values when doing so disrupts your company's earning power and your own career ascent. It takes courage to pull back judiciously and deliberately, "to figure out how to make a contribution to the world that feels both authentic and well within your human limits," as essayist Rosie Spinks writes, "to participate in an energetic exchange that isn't predicated on burnout or a ceaseless expectation of more."

It's easier to summon this kind of courage (or stubbornness, as the case may be) when you surround yourself with the off-course equivalent of a runner's pacing team: people who are making authentic contributions untethered to one-upmanship, who reject cultural norms that equate grind with virtue, and who create abundance that has nothing to do with their job title or account balance. These fellow travelers' influence is contagious. When you witness others calling out lapses in integrity, you, too, will be more drawn to honest reckoning, recognizing when your bodily, mental, or ethical integrity has broken down and taking steps to restore it.

For Michele Benoit, figuring out how to make her own meaningful contribution felt a bit like learning a new language. After she decided to pursue coaching, her life didn't get less busy right away. In some ways, in fact, it got busier, since her schedule had to accommodate the training courses she needed to get certified, and soon, handle a growing stable of coaching clients.

Yet Benoit felt more in control of everything she was doing, more certain she was putting her talents to best use. And because of that, she wasted less mental energy wondering what others thought of her plans. "When people challenge me," she says, "I'm like, 'It is what it is. You may understand it, you may not.'"

The choices that have steered Benoit toward flourishing also feel more manageable on a granular level each day. "There are a lot of small things that are different because I have the capacity now," she says. She wakes up without an alarm clock because she's no longer running short on sleep. She goes on daily hour-plus walks in New York's Central Park. And she stops to have leisurely chats with people without mentally accounting for time lost.

Refashioning her life into a cohesive whole has given Benoit so much more space, both mental and practical, that she no longer needs to hoard the few minutes on the margins. This is the essence of pacing: noticing when frantic sprints or drawn-out stalls are consuming you—not just physically but ethically and existentially—and making bold adjustments that heal and strengthen you on every level.

Acknowledgments

From the first weeks of this project's gestation, my editors and the team at Simon & Schuster have seen me through. I'm so grateful to Leah Miller for being among the first to see this book's potential and for convincing me it could be a force for good. Kimberly Meilun was instrumental in guiding me through nearly the entire process of creating the book, urging me onward and nudging me back on course when I drifted off. I can't imagine a better pacing partner in a long-haul venture like this.

My agent, Susan Canavan, has been much more than a helper and cheerleader through the bookmaking process—she is truly a co-creator. It was Susan who got me thinking about all the unexpected dimensions of pacing, and we went on to discuss the topic in ways that helped me form the genesis of this book. It is no exaggeration to say that, without her, it would not exist.

Four years ago, I made one of the best decisions of my life: joining the Writers Grotto in San Francisco, which supports creativity, creators, and the arts at a time when they face unprecedented assault. I'm indebted to Rebecca Black, Julia Scheeres, Jesus Sierra, Brad Balukjian, Pia Chatterjee, Saila Kariat, Audrey Ferber, Jenny Qi, Alissa Greenberg, Thaisa Frank, and so many other Grotto-ites who have offered encouragement in writing and in life. Your friendship and support keep me at this solitary grind day after day.

The members of my "Jersey Knit Goals" writers' group—Lauren Gravitz, Rebecca Boyle, Cassandra Willyard, Emily Sohn, and Hannah

Hoag—have listened and counseled me through each phase of this project, reassuring me through twists and turns that made it hard to see more than a few feet ahead. I'm also grateful to Georgia Platts and Ilona Merli, writers and changemakers who've encouraged me since they first heard about "the pacing book"; to Jeremy Adam Smith, my editor at *Greater Good Magazine*, with whom I first delved into some of the ideas in the book; and to Hamada Salem, who supplied vital research assistance when I was in a time crunch (perhaps failing to pace myself). To the dozens of scientists, athletes, and fellow travelers I interviewed over the course of more than two years: This book would be an insubstantial shadow without your input and generosity.

Finally, I want to thank the three humans—small and large—with whom I share a home, a life, and a growing list of Simpsons references. Your questions about what pacing looks like, and what it means when you're not running a race, pushed me to think more deeply and express myself more clearly. My thoughts coalesced on the page thanks to your willingness to let me escape on self-imposed writing retreats. Your love, now and always, helps me to set a sustaining pace.

Notes

Introduction

1   *As the early sun glints through a scrim of trees:* Author observations here and throughout chapter are at the Boston Trail Half Marathon, Elizabeth Township, Pennsylvania, April 12–13, 2024.

1   *veteran marathoner Crist and his handpicked pacing team:* Jim Crist, interviews with author.

1   *Fifteen minutes before the starting gun:* Elijah Shekinah and Mike Salamon, interviews with author.

6   *"We don't learn how to pace ourselves":* Emily Masters Rosenthal, interview with author, August 2023.

9   *Rollo May defines freedom:* Rollo May, *Freedom and Destiny* (W. W. Norton, 1999), 54.

Chapter 1: A Breakneck Pace

13   *riding an ever-looping conveyor belt:* Sarah Fisher, "The Burnout Epidemic, or Why I Wrote This Article at Midnight the Day after the Deadline," *Trinitonian,* November 18, 2022, https://trinitonian.com/2022/11/18/finals-and-burnout/.

13   *At her public high school in Nashville, Tennessee:* Sarah Fisher, interview with author, September 2024.

13   *"the excitement of competition, the charm of anticipated success":* Alexis de Tocqueville, *Democracy in America,* vol. 2 (Antigonos, 2025), 105.

14   *"and nothing exterior shall ever take command of me":* Walt Whitman, *Leaves of Grass* (Boni & Liveright, 1921), 156.

14   *automation and offshoring conspired to eliminate millions of jobs:* US Congress, House Committee on Foreign Affairs. Subcommittee on

International Economic Policy and Trade, *A New Framework for Global Growth in the 1990's: Hearings Before the Subcommittee on International Economic Policy and Trade of the Committee on Foreign Affairs, House of Representatives, One Hundredth Congress, Second Session, May 19 and September 29, 1988*, vol. 4 (US Government Printing Office, 1989).

14   *"the purpose of life becomes the accumulation of gold stars"*: William Deresiewicz, *Excellent Sheep: The Miseducation of the American Elite and the Way to a Meaningful Life* (Free Press, 2014), 16.

14   *"The five kids in our family were never pushed"*: Mary Westheimer, interview with author, August and September 2024.

15   *Her grueling elite training regimen, she explained:* Karen Crouse, "Gracie Gold's Battle for Olympic Glory Ended in a Fight to Save Herself," *New York Times*, January 25, 2019, https://www.nytimes.com/2019/01/25/sports/gracie-gold-figure-skating-.html.

15   *Three in ten kids have perfectionism:* Amanda Sironic and Robert A. Reeve, "A Combined Analysis of the Frost Multidimensional Perfectionism Scale (FMPS), Child and Adolescent Perfectionism Scale (CAPS), and Almost Perfect Scale–Revised (APS-R): Different Perfectionist Profiles in Adolescent High School Students," *Psychological Assessment* 27, no. 4 (2015): 1471–83, https://doi.org/10.1037/pas0000137.

15   *2023 Gallup poll of more than 2,400 college students:* Zach Hrynowski and Stephanie Marken, "College Students Experience High Levels of Worry and Stress," Gallup, August 10, 2023, https://www.gallup.com/education/509231/college-students-experience-high-levels-worry-stress.aspx.

15   *leading them to consider dropping:* Stephanie Marken, "Black, Hispanic Students at Greatest Risk of Leaving Program," Gallup, February 28, 2024, https://news.gallup.com/poll/611093/black-hispanic-students-greatest-risk-leaving-program.aspx.

18   *The editor and poet Devrupa Rakshit struggles to relax:* Devrupa Rakshit, "Is This Normal? 'I Hate Relaxing,'" *The Swaddle*, October 21, 2022, https://www.theswaddle.com/is-this-normal-i-hate-relaxing.

18   *"feels as if you're muddling through your days":* Adam Grant, "There's a Name for the Blah You're Feeling: It's Called Languishing," *New York Times*, April 19, 2021, https://www.nytimes.com/2021/04/19/well/mind/covid-mental-health-languishing.html.

19   *She's seen it countless times before:* Christina Maslach, interview with author, May 2023.

19   *High levels of early-life stress, research shows:* Eric M. Brown, Kristy L. Carlisle, Melanie Burgess, Jacob Clark, and Hariel Hutcheon, "Adverse and Positive Childhood Experiences of Clinical Mental Health Counselors as Predictors of Compassion Satisfaction, Burnout, and Secondary Traumatic Stress," *Professional Counselor* 12, no. 1 (2022): 49–64, https://doi.org/10.15241/emb.12.1.49.

19   *more likely to crash and burn:* Annika Evolahti, Daniel Hultell, and Aila Collins, "Development of Burnout in Middle-Aged Working Women: A Longitudinal Study," *Journal of Women's Health* 22, no. 1 (2013): 94–103, https://doi.org/10.1089/jwh.2012.3507.

19   *the quintessential society that never sleeps:* Sandee LaMotte, "Sleep Deprivation Affects Nearly Half of American Adults, Study Finds," CNN, November 8, 2022, https://www.cnn.com/2022/11/08/health/sleep-deprivation-wellness/index.html.

19   *employees who work seventy hours a week:* John H. Pencavel, *The Productivity of Working Hours*, IZA Discussion Paper No. 8129 (Institute of Labor Economics, 2014), https://docs.iza.org/dp8129.pdf.

19   *more likely to get injured at work:* Kapo Wong, Alan H. S. Chan, and Stephen C. K. Ngan, "The Effect of Long Working Hours and Overtime on Occupational Health: A Meta-Analysis of Evidence from 1998 to 2018," *International Journal of Environmental Research and Public Health* 16, no. 12 (2019): Article 2102, https://doi.org/10.3390/ijerph16122102.

20   *"The language of winning and losing exhausts us":* Francesco Duina, *Winning: Reflections on an American Obsession* (Princeton University Press, 2013).

20   *the kind of reflection that fuels engaged activism:* Jenny Odell, *How to Do Nothing: Resisting the Attention Economy* (Melville House, 2019), 22.

21   *Rested people also have greater cognitive flexibility:* K. A. Honn, J. M. Hinson, P. Whitney, and H. P. A. Van Dongen, "Cognitive Flexibility: A Distinct Element of Performance Impairment Due to Sleep Deprivation," *Accident Analysis & Prevention* 126 (May 2019): 191–97, https://doi.org/10.1016/j.aap.2018.02.013.

21   *find life meaningful and satisfying:* William Killgore et al., "Sleep Quality and Self-Perceived Flourishing in Life," *Sleep* 47, Suppl. 1 (2024): A407, https://doi.org/10.1093/sleep/zsae067.0949.

21   *the more motivated you'll feel:* Patrick E. McKnight and Todd B. Kashdan, "Purpose in Life as a System that Creates and Sustains Health and Well-

Being: An Integrative, Testable Theory," *Review of General Psychology* 13, no. 3 (2009): 242–51, https://doi.org/10.1037/a0017152.

21 *For insight into setting this elusive rhythm:* Amy Baltzell, chats with author, January–April 2023.

22 *can seem like the only attainable bright spots:* Naomi Klein, *Doppelganger: A Trip Into the Mirror World* (Farrar, Straus and Giroux, 2023).

22 *more than 30 percent remained clinically exhausted:* Kristina Glise, Lilian Wiegner, and Ingibjörg H. Jonsdottir, "Long-Term Follow-up of Residual Symptoms in Patients Treated for Stress-Related Exhaustion," *BMC Psychology* 8, no. 26 (2020), https://doi.org/10.1186/s40359-020-0395-8.

24 *Max Weber's "unalterable order of things":* Victor Jeleniewski Seidler, *Recovering the Self: Morality and Social Theory* (Taylor & Francis, 2013), 47.

Chapter 2: A Biological Reckoning

25 *The oldest daughter of Indian immigrant parents:* Patty Johnson, interviews with author, September 2024–May 2025.

27 *potent cocktail of stress hormones:* Howard E. LeWine, "Understanding the Stress Response," *Harvard Health Publishing*, April 3, 2024, https://www.health.harvard.edu/staying-healthy/understanding-the-stress-response.

27 *Signs of the toll this state takes are subtle at first:* David Rabin, interview with author, December 2022.

27 *Accumulation of arterial plaque:* Bo-chen Yao, Ling-bing Meng, and Zhigang Guo, "Chronic Stress: A Critical Risk Factor for Atherosclerosis," *Journal of International Medical Research* 47, no. 4 (2019): 1429–40, https://doi.org/10.1177/0300060519826820.

27 *California State University survey:* Robert V. Levine and Ara Norenzayan, "The Pace of Life in 31 Countries," *Journal of Cross-Cultural Psychology* 30, no. 2 (1999): 178–205, https://doi.org/10.1177/0022022199030002003.

28 *end up in poorer overall health by their thirties:* A. K. Farrell, J. A Simpson, E. A. Carlson, M. M. Englund, and S. Sung, "The Impact of Stress at Different Life Stages on Physical Health and the Buffering Effects of Maternal Sensitivity," *Health Psychology* 36, no. 1 (2017): 35–44, https://doi.org/10.1037/hea0000424.

28 *people of color report higher stress levels:* Elizabeth Brondolo, Kahaema Byer, Peter J. Gianaros, Cindy Liu, Aric A. Prather, et al., *Stress and Health Disparities: Contexts, Mechanisms, and Interventions Among Racial/Ethnic*

Minority and Low Socioeconomic Status Populations (American Psychological Association, 2017), https://www.apa.org/pi/health-equity/resources/stress-report.

29 *interferes with the brain's executive function:* Tamara Cibrian-Llanderal, Montserrat Melgarejo-Gutierrez, and Daniel Hernandez-Baltazar, "Stress and Cognition: Psychological Basis and Support Resources," in *Health and Academic Achievement*, ed. Blandina Bernal-Morales (IntechOpen, 2018), https://www.intechopen.com/chapters/59046.

29 *scanned the brains of more than one hundred people:* I. Savic, A. Perski, and W. Osika, "MRI Shows that Exhaustion Syndrome Due to Chronic Occupational Stress Is Associated with Partially Reversible Cerebral Changes," *Cerebral Cortex* 28, no. 3 (2018): 894–906, https://doi.org/10.1093/cercor/bhw413.

29 *anyone with a history of mental health struggles:* Sean Haugh, interview with author, October 2023.

29 *certain neurons in the midbrain:* Kafui Dzirasa, "Neuronal Suppression Causing Depression?," *Science Translational Medicine* 10, no. 425 (2018): eaar7520, https://doi.org/10.1126/scitranslmed.aar7520.

30 *prolonged stress inhibits flourishing:* Daisuke Hori et al., "Association Between Flourishing Mental Health and Occupational Stress Among Workers of Tsukuba Science City, Japan: A Cross-Sectional Study," *Environmental Health and Preventive Medicine* 24, no. 1 (2019), https://doi.org/10.1186/s12199-019-0823-7.

30 *David Rabin:* David Rabin, interview with author, December 2022.

31 *can stem from prolonged stress:* Rachel Lampert et al., "Cumulative Stress and Autonomic Dysregulation in a Community Sample," *Stress* 19, no. 3 (2016): 269–79, https://doi.org/10.1080/10253890.2016.1174847.

31 *"more like a Maserati than a Volkswagen":* Joseph Arpaia, interview with author, November 2022.

32 *stress that triggers physical and mental upset:* Erika Lutin et al., "The Cumulative Effect of Chronic Stress and Depressive Symptoms Affects Heart Rate in a Working Population," *Frontiers in Psychiatry* 13 (October 13, 2022), https://doi.org/10.3389/fpsyt.2022.1022298.

32 *the pituitary gland signals the adrenal glands:* Lauren Thau, Jayashree Gandhi, and Sandeep Sharma, "Physiology, Cortisol," in *StatPearls* (StatPearls Publishing, 2023), https://www.ncbi.nlm.nih.gov/books/NB538239/.

32 *a variety of abnormal cortisol-release patterns:* Emilija Knezevic, Katarina Nenic, Vladislav Milanovic, and Nebojsa Nick Knezevic, "The Role of Cortisol in Chronic Stress, Neurodegenerative Diseases, and Psychological Disorders," *Cells* 12, no. 23 (2023): 2726, https://doi.org/10.3390/cells12232726.

33 *Massachusetts interior designer Hannah Oravec:* Hannah Oravec, interview with author, September 2024.

34 *Maslach Burnout Inventory:* Christina Maslach, Susan E. Jackson, and Michael P. Leiter, eds., *Maslach Burnout Inventory Manual*, 3rd ed. (Consulting Psychologists Press, 1996).

35 *twice as likely:* Denise Albieri Jodas Salvagioni et al., "Physical, Psychological and Occupational Consequences of Job Burnout: A Systematic Review of Prospective Studies," *PLoS One* 12, no. 10 (2017): e0185781, https://doi.org/10.1371/journal.pone.0185781.

36 *"Not to be flexible and malleable":* Daryl Appleton, interview with author, April 2023.

Chapter 3: Plotting a Narrative Arc

39 *Jony M. Weiss was no stranger:* Jony Weiss, interview with author, September 2024.

40 *"One of the primary ways that we find meaning":* Ben Rogers, interview with author, January 2024.

41 *the human desire to locate themes in life:* Milan Kundera, *The Unbearable Lightness of Being*, trans. Michael Henry Heim (Harper & Row, 1984).

41 *without a clear sense of why he wanted to live on:* Viktor E. Frankl, *Man's Search for Meaning*, trans. Ilse Lasch (Beacon Press, 2006).

41 *"my mind clung to my wife's image":* Ibid., 57.

42 *asked people to tell a story:* Brady Jones, Mesmin Destin, and Dan P. McAdams, "Telling Better Stories: Competence-Building Narrative Themes Increase Adolescent Persistence and Academic Achievement," *Journal of Experimental Social Psychology* 76 (May 2018): 76–80, https://doi.org/10.1016/j.jesp.2017.12.006.

42 *Some of my conversations with Amy Baltzell:* Amy Baltzell, chats with author, January–April 2023.

44 *they found their lives more meaningful:* Ben A. Rogers et al., "Seeing Your Life Story as a Hero's Journey Increases Meaning in Life," *Journal of Per-*

sonality and Social Psychology 125, no. 4 (2023): 752–78, https://doi.org /10.1037/pspa0000341.

48   *novelist James Baldwin told an interviewer:* Jane Howard, "Telling Talk from a Negro Writer," *LIFE* magazine, 54, no. 21 (May 24, 1963), 81–92, 100–102.

48   *In a Texas A&M study:* William E. Davis, Nicholas J. Kelley, Jinhyung Kim, David Tang, and Joshua A. Hicks, "Motivating the Academic Mind: High-Level Construal of Academic Goals Enhances Goal Meaningfulness, Motivation, and Self-Concordance," *Motivation and Emotion* 40, no. 2 (2015): 193–202, https://doi.org/10.1007/s11031-015-9522-x.

49   *better able to handle periodic stress:* Arnold Bakker, "A Job Demands–Resources Approach to Public Service Motivation," *Public Administration Review* 75, no. 5 (2015): 723–32, https://doi.org/10.1111/puar.12388.

50   *a Claire Vaye Watkins essay:* Claire Vaye Watkins, "On Pandering," *Tin House,* November 23, 2015, https://tinhouse.com/on-pandering/.

50   *asked people to tell the story of their life:* Theodore E. A. Waters, Christin Köber, Tilmann Haberman, and Robyn Fivush, "Consistency and Stability of Narrative Coherence: An Examination of Personal Narrative as a Domain of Adult Personality," *Journal of Personality* 87, no. 2 (2018): 151–62, https://onlinelibrary.wiley.com/doi/10.1111/jopy.12377.

Chapter 4: Find Your Pulse

55   *an unusually warm day in May:* Ajeé Wilson, interview with author, May 2024.

56   *"response flexibility":* Gabor Maté and Daniel Maté, *The Myth of Normal: Trauma, Illness & Healing in a Toxic Culture* (Penguin Random House, 2022).

56   *writes performance psychologist Jim Loehr:* Jim Loehr and Tony Schwartz, *The Power of Full Engagement: Managing Energy, Not Time, Is the Key to High Performance and Personal Renewal* (Free Press, 2003), 12.

57   *midmorning and midafternoon breaks:* Juliet B. Schor, *The Overworked American: The Unexpected Decline of Leisure* (Basic Books, 1992), 46.

57   *what he called "natural chronology":* Christoph Wilhelm Hufeland, *Hufeland's Art of Prolonging Life* (Lindsay & Blakiston, 1867).

57   *"No time clock daunts the coffee-breakers":* "Manners & Morals: The Coffee Hour," *Time,* March 5, 1951, https://time.com/archive/6608068/manners -morals-the-coffee-hour/.

58   *banging out "pomodoros":* Pomodoro Technique, accessed July 18, 2025, https://www.pomodorotechnique.com/.

58   *"The era of time management has passed":* Colleen Hacker, interview with author, October 2022.

59   *a few hours after awakening:* Pablo Valdez, "Circadian Rhythms in Attention," *Yale Journal of Biology and Medicine* 92, no. 1 (2019): 81–92, https://pmc.ncbi.nlm.nih.gov/articles/PMC6430172/.

59   *about one or two hours at a time:* David Kaiser, "Infralow Frequencies and Ultradian Rhythms," *Seminars in Pediatric Neurology* 20, no. 4 (2013): 242–45, https://doi.org/10.1016/j.spen.2013.10.005.

60   *New York City real estate broker Nikki Beauchamp:* Nikki Beauchamp, interview with author, August 2024.

61   *more than thirty thousand Americans' daily routines:* Marissa A. Sharif, Cassie Mogilner, and Hal E. Hershfield, "Having Too Little or Too Much Time Is Linked to Lower Subjective Well-Being," *Journal of Personality and Social Psychology* 121, no. 4 (2021): 933–47, https://pubmed.ncbi.nlm.nih.gov/34498892/.

61   *taking on measured amounts of "eustress":* Sandor Szabo, Yvette Tache, and Arpad Somogyi, "The Legacy of Hans Selye and the Origins of Stress Research," *Stress* 15, no. 5 (2012): 472–78, https://doi.org/10.3109/10253890.2012.710919.

62   *Too much slack time:* Cassie Holmes, "'Too Much Free Time Won't Make You Happier,' Says Psychologist—How Many Hours You Really Need in a Day," *CNBC Make It*, September 12, 2022, https://www.cnbc.com/2022/09/08/too-much-free-time-wont-make-you-happier-says-psychologist-how-many-hours-you-really-need-in-a-day.html.

62   *under-the-gun sense of time pressure:* Don A. Moore and Elizabeth R. Tenney, "Time Pressure, Performance, and Productivity," in *Looking Back, Moving Forward: A Review of Group and Team-Based Research*, ed. Margaret A. Neale and Elizabeth A. Mannix, Research on Managing Groups and Teams 15 (Emerald Group Publishing, 2012), 305–26, https://doi.org/10.1108/S1534-0856(2012)0000015015.

63   *a study of breaks lasting ten minutes or less:* Patricia Albulescu et al., "'Give Me a Break!' A Systematic Review and Meta-Analysis on the Efficacy of Micro-Breaks for Increasing Well-Being and Performance," *PLoS One* 17, no. 8 (2022): e0272460, https://doi.org/10.1371/journal.pone.0272460.

63 *the more say people have:* Marjaana Sianoja, Ulla Kinnunen, Jessica de Bloom, Kalevi Korpela, and Savine Geurta, "Recovery During Lunch Breaks: Testing Long-Term Relations with Energy Levels at Work," *Scandinavian Journal of Work and Organizational Psychology* 1, no. 1 (2016): 7, https://doi.org/10.16993/sjwop.13.

64 *In a Norwegian study of cross-country skiers:* Espen Tønnessen et al., "The Road to Gold: Training and Peaking Characteristics in the Year Prior to a Gold Medal Endurance Performance," *PLoS One* 9, no. 7 (2014): e101796, https://doi.org/10.1371/journal.pone.0101796.

64 *two to four hours of creatively demanding work:* Alex S. Pang, "Why Science Benefits When We Think More and Do Less," *Psychology Today*, September 2, 2015, https://www.psychologytoday.com/us/blog/rest/201509/why -science-benefits-when-we-think-more-and-do-less.

64 *a survey of nearly two thousand office workers:* "Survey Reveals Employee Productivity Averages 2 Hours and 53 Minutes a Day," Vouchercloud, January 22, 2018, https://www.vouchercloud.com/better-living/office-worker -productivity.

65 *which reliably improves performance:* Zhiqiang Wang, Yong "Tai" Wang, Weifeng Gao, and Yaping Zhong, "Effects of Tapering on Performance in Endurance Athletes: A Systematic Review and Meta-Analysis," *PLoS One* 18, no. 5 (2023): e0282838, https://doi.org/10.1371/journal.pone .0282838.

65 *an approach called "periodization":* "Central Concepts Related to Periodization," National Strength and Conditioning Association, May 2017, https:// www.nsca.com/education/articles/kinetic-select/central-concepts-related -to-periodization/.

65 *less stressed and more satisfied on the job:* Tapas K. Ray and Regina Pana-Cryan, "Work Flexibility and Work-Related Well-Being," *International Journal of Environmental Research and Public Health* 18, no. 6 (2021): 3254, https://doi.org/10.3390/ijerph18063254.

66 *often practice "activity pacing":* Martin Ackah, Vincent Deary, Ulric S. Abonie, Florentina J. Hettinga, and Katie L. Hackett, "'Rest Recharges My Energy'; Experiences and Perceptions of Rest in Adults with Long-Term Conditions and Fatigue in Rehabilitation: A Qualitative Study," *Disability and Rehabilitation*, June 3, 2025, 1–12, https://doi.org/10.1080 /09638288.2025.2512587.

Chapter 5: The Art of Modulation

69   *When Joe Arpaia was in medical school:* Joseph Arpaia, interviews with author, September and November 2022.

70   *training them to practice what he called "unease modulation":* Joseph Arpaia and Judith P. Andersen, "The Unease Modulation Model: An Experiential Model of Stress with Implications for Health, Stress Management, and Public Policy," *Frontiers in Psychiatry* 10 (June 7, 2019), https://doi.org/10.3389/fpsyt.2019.00379.

72   *Wade Warren, a retired vet and probation officer:* Wade Warren, interview with author, September 2024.

77   *In one Brigham Young University study:* Patrick R. Steffen, Tara Austin, Andrea DeBarros, and Tracy Brown, "The Impact of Resonance Frequency Breathing on Measures of Heart Rate Variability, Blood Pressure, and Mood," *Frontiers in Public Health* 5 (August 25, 2017), https://doi.org/10.3389/fpubh.2017.00222.

78   *twenty straight minutes of daily resonant frequency breathing:* Shyam Chaitanya, Anjum Datta, Bharti Bhandari, and Vivek Kumar Sharma, "Effect of Resonance Breathing on Heart Rate Variability and Cognitive Functions in Young Adults: A Randomised Controlled Study," *Cureus*, February 13, 2022, https://doi.org/10.7759/cureus.22187.

78   *a weeks-long course in modulation skills:* Judith P. Andersen, Joseph Arpaia, Harri Gustafsberg, Steve Poplawski, and Paula M. DiNota, "The International Performance, Resilience and Efficiency Program Protocol for the Application of HRV Biofeedback in Applied Law Enforcement Settings," *Applied Psychophysiology and Biofeedback* 49, no. 3 (2024): 483–502, https://doi.org/10.1007/s10484-024-09644-3.

Chapter 6: Digital Triage

85   *As the year 2023 drew to a close:* Noelle Frost, interview with author, September 2024.

85   *cycle of engagement she calls the "ludic loop":* Natasha Dow Schüll, *Addiction by Design: Machine Gambling in Las Vegas* (Princeton University Press, 2014).

85   *their brains flood with dopamine:* Barbara Jacquelyn Sahakian, Christelle Langley, Henrietta Bowden-Jones, and Sara Chamberlain, "Gambling: What Happens in the Brain When We Get Hooked—and How to Regain

Control," *The Conversation*, February 16, 2022, https://theconversation
.com/gambling-what-happens-in-the-brain-when-we-get-hooked-and
-how-to-regain-control-176901.

86 *"We gorge on social media":* Carl Honoré, interview with author, March 2024.

87 *received likes on an app similar to Instagram:* Lauren E. Sherman, Patricia M.
Greenfield, Leanna M. Hernandez, and Mirella Dapretto, "Peer Influence
via Instagram: Effects on Brain and Behavior in Adolescence and Young
Adulthood," *Child Development* 89, no. 1 (2017): 37–47, https://doi.org
/10.1111/cdev.12838.

87 *when gamblers view pictures of slot machines:* E. H. Limbrick-Oldfield,
H. Bowden-Jones, D. Nutt, A. Lingford-Hughes, and L. Clark, "Neural Sub-
strates of Cue Reactivity and Craving in Gambling Disorder," *Translational
Psychiatry* 7, no. 1 (2017): e992, https://doi.org/10.1038/tp.2016.256.

87 *started to activate while they were anticipating:* Wolfram Schultz, Paul Api-
cella, and Tomas Ljungberg, "Responses of Monkey Dopamine Neurons
to Reward and Conditioned Stimuli During Successive Steps of Learning a
Delayed Response Task," *Journal of Neuroscience* 13, no. 3 (1993): 900–13,
https://doi.org/10.1523/JNEUROSCI.13-03-00900.1993.

87 *Programmers deliberately evoke users' anger:* Luke Munn, "Angry by Design:
Toxic Communication and Technical Architectures," *Humanities and
Social Sciences Communications* 7, no. 1 (2020), https://doi.org/10.1057
/s41599-020-00550-7.

88 *"looking at my phone hundreds of times per day":* John Green, "I Decided to
Take a Year off from Social Media. Here's What I've Learned So Far," *Washington Post,* January 23, 2019, https://www.washingtonpost.com/opinions
/i-decided-to-take-a-year-off-from-social-media-heres-what-ive-learned
-so-far/2019/01/23/714a0e7a-1e53-11e9-9145-3f74070bbdb9_story.html.

88 *poorer long-term memory:* Melina R. Uncapher and Anthony D. Wagner,
"Minds and Brains of Media Multitaskers: Current Findings and Future
Directions," *Proceedings of the National Academy of Sciences* 115, no. 40
(2018): 9889–96, https://doi.org/10.1073/pnas.1611612115.

88 *twice as likely as lighter users:* Jean M. Twenge and W. Keith Campbell,
"Media Use Is Linked to Lower Psychological Well-Being: Evidence from
Three Datasets," *Psychiatric Quarterly* 90, no. 2 (2019): 311–31, https://doi
.org/10.1007/s11126-019-09630-7.

89 *explained in an Instagram post:* Emily St. Martin, "Chris Evans and Taron
Egerton Deactivate Socials: 'My Ability to Be Present Is Eroding,'" *Los*

Angeles Times, June 30, 2023, https://www.latimes.com/entertainment
-arts/story/2023-06-30/chris-evans-taron-egerton-deactivate-social-media
-bad-bunny-twitter-instagram-delete-account.

89 *taking a monthlong social media break:* "A New Years Experiment: One
Month Without Social Media," *Noelle Across the Pond* (blog), February 12, 2024, https://noelleacrossthepond.com/2024/02/12/a-new-years
-experiment-one-month-without-social-media/.

90 *studied digital limit setting in an experiment:* Jackie Silverman, Jordan Etkin,
and Shalena Srna, *Can Time Limits Increase Time Spent?* Marketing Science
Institute Working Paper No. 24152 (Marketing Science Institute, 2024),
https://www.msi.org/working-paper/can-time-limits-increase-time-spent/.

91 *how entrenched my digital habits have become:* Amy Baltzell, chats with author, January–April 2023.

92 *often works better than banishing the first habit:* "Healthy, Active, and Sustainable Commuting Intervention: An Intervention Study to Examine
Habit Substitution of Commuting Habits," German Clinical Trials Register (DRKS00028479), registered March 24, 2022, last updated December 13, 2023, https://drks.de/search/en/trial/DRKS00028479.

92 *"I've curated my social feeds":* Montrez Williams, interview with author, August 2024.

93 *University of Houston study:* Vanessa M. Patrick and Henrik Hagtvedt,
"'I Don't' versus 'I Can't': When Empowered Refusal Motivates Goal-
Directed Behavior," *Journal of Consumer Research* 39, no. 2 (2012):
371–81, https://doi.org/10.1086/663212.

93 *"I stopped looking at my phone":* Jenny Odell, *How to Do Nothing: Resisting
the Attention Economy* (Melville House, 2019), 184.

94 *he posted a series of TikToks:* Carlos De Loera, "World Cup: For Author John
Green, TikToks Are Another Way to Show His Love of Soccer," *Los Angeles
Times*, December 16, 2022, https://www.latimes.com/sports/soccer/story
/2022-12-16/john-green-world-cup-tiktok.

94 *He's also made YouTube videos:* John Green, "How We End TB," Vlogbroth-
ers, YouTube video, 5:14, March 12, 2024, https://www.youtube.com
/watch?v=s03XSN1F-BY.

94 *"This is the middle of history":* "Why 'Everything Is Tuberculosis' with
John Green," MSNBC, April 7, 2025, https://www.msnbc.com/msnbc
-podcast/why-is-this-happening/withpod-everything-tuberculosis
-john-green-rcna199319.

95 *setting customized alerts that pop up:* "Pause Before Opening a Distracting App," ScreenZen (website), accessed July 18, 2025, https://www.screen zen.co.

95 *the kinds of content streams that draw eyeballs:* Kevin Tran, "People Have Become Pickier About What They Post to Social Media," *Morning Consult*, October 17, 2023, https://pro.morningconsult.com/analysis/social-media -posting-frequency-preferences-survey.

95 *a tidal wave of so-called AI slop:* Jon Roozenbeek, Sander van der Linden, and Yara Kyrychenko, "What Is AI Slop? Why You Are Seeing More Fake Photos and Videos in Your Social Media Feeds," *The Conversation*, May 28, 2025, https://theconversation.com/what-is-ai-slop-why-you-are-seeing-more -fake-photos-and-videos-in-your-social-media-feeds-255538.

95 *ten fewer minutes on social media each day in late 2024:* Simon Kemp, "Digital 2025: The Essential Guide to the Global State of Digital," *We Are Social* (blog), February 5, 2025, https://wearesocial.com/us/blog/2025/02 /digital-2025-the-essential-guide-to-the-global-state-of-digital/.

Chapter 7: Flourishing in Flow

97 *Alannah Yip chalked her hands:* Alannah Yip, interview with author, May 2023.

98 *as Csikszentmihalyi explained before his death:* Mihaly Csikszentmihalyi, "Flow, the Secret to Happiness," TED video, February 2004, https://www .ted.com/talks/mihaly_csikszentmihalyi_flow_the_secret_to_happiness.

98 *Studies show a high degree of connection:* Richard Huskey et al., "Flexible and Modular Brain Network Dynamics Characterize Flow Experiences During Media Use: A Functional Magnetic Resonance Imaging Study," *Journal of Communication* 72, no. 1 (2021): 6–32, https://doi.org/10.1093 /joc/jqab044.

98 *offers managers a detailed road map:* "Flow State: A Gateway to Engagement, Performance, and Productivity," McLean & Company, May 10, 2023, https://hr.mcleanco.com/research/ss/flow-state-a-gateway-to -engagement-performance-and-productivity.

98 *"Flow State: Unlock Your Superhuman Productivity":* Jim Kwik, "Flow State: Unlock Your Superhuman Productivity," Jim Kwik, YouTube video, 7:35, November 13, 2023, https://www.youtube.com/watch?v= s5GwCqOFwNA.

98 *pursuits that engage you in and of themselves:* Palav Mehta and Mahimna Vyas, "A Systematic Literature Review on the Experience of Flow and Its Relation to Intrinsic Motivation in Students," *Indian Journal of Positive Psychology* 13, no. 3 (2022): 299–304, https://www.researchgate.net/publication/364344204_A_Systematic_Literature_Review_on_the_Experience_of_Flow_and_its_Relation_to_Intrinsic_Motivation_in_Students.

99 *the violinist Diane Allen says, "your work refuels you":* Diane Allen, interview with author, July 2023.

99 *"moving into a separate reality, temporarily":* "In Conversation with Mihaly Csikszentmihalyi at Happiness & Its Causes 2014," moderated by Richard Fidler, YouTube video, 31:29, August 19, 2014, https://www.youtube.com/watch?v=lSPFadWJDXE.

99 *Climbing, he told a writer:* Peter Mayfield, "A Climber We Lost: Mihaly Csikszentmihalyi, October 10," *Climbing,* January 4, 2022, https://www.climbing.com/people/a-climber-we-lost-mihaly-csikszentmihalyi/.

99 *who worked in the same way their ancestors had:* Mihaly Csikszentmihalyi, *Flow: The Psychology of Optimal Experience* (Harper & Row, 1990).

100 *Czikszentmihalyi reflected in one interview:* John Geirland, "Go with the Flow," *Wired,* September 1, 1996, https://www.wired.com/1996/09/czik/.

100 *"With a little bit of effort":* Sam Spurlin, "How to Build More Flow into Your Work Day," SamSpurlin.com (blog), January 3, 2020, https://www.samspurlin.com/blog/how-to-build-more-flow.

101 *when they do things they actually enjoy:* Mehta and Vyas, "Systematic Literature Review."

101 *"you'll have a hard time losing yourself in it":* Leo Babauta, "9 Steps to Achieving Flow in Your Work," DailyGood, April 30, 2012, https://www.dailygood.org/story/224/9-steps-to-achieving-flow-in-your-work-leo-babauta/.

101 *scanned the brains of improv jazz musicians:* Charles J. Limb and Allen R. Braun, "Neural Substrates of Spontaneous Musical Performance: An FMRI Study of Jazz Improvisation," *PLoS One* 3, no. 2 (2008): e1679, https://doi.org/10.1371/journal.pone.0001679.

101 *in part because it blots out self-awareness:* Darius Parvizi-Wayne et al., "Forgetting Ourselves in Flow: An Active Inference Account of Flow States and How We Experience Ourselves within Them," *Frontiers in Psychology* 15 (June 3, 2024), https://doi.org/10.3389/fpsyg.2024.1354719.

102 *A surer route to flourishing is ego erasure:* Guanyu Liu, Linda M. Isbell, Michael J. Constantino, and Bernhard Leidner, "Quiet Ego Intervention Enhances Flourishing by Increasing Quiet Ego Characteristics and Trait Emotional Intelligence: A Randomized Experiment," *Journal of Happiness Studies* 23, no. 7 (2022): 3605–23, https://doi.org/10.1007/s10902-022 -00560-z.

104 *just a hair past your current abilities:* Dimitri van der Linden, Mattie Tops, and Arnold B. Bakker, "The Neuroscience of the Flow State: Involvement of the Locus Coeruleus Norepinephrine System," *Frontiers in Psychology* 12 (April 14, 2021), https://doi.org/10.3389/fpsyg.2021.645498.

105 *In his conception of the "Breakout Principle":* Herbert Benson and William Proctor, *The Breakout Principle: How to Activate the Natural Trigger That Maximizes Creativity, Athletic Performance, Productivity and Personal Well-Being* (Simon & Schuster, 2003).

107 *Tinfow has guarded what he calls his "cloistered time":* Randall Tinfow, interview with author, December 2024.

108 *Cola started reserving sixty to ninety minutes a day:* Martina Cola, interview with author, December 2024.

108 *one Taiwanese study of eighty-four full-time employees:* Wan-Jing April Chang, Ya-Jen Cheng, and Kuo-Yang Kao, "The Mediating Role of Flow State Between Recovery and Energy Levels: An Experience Sampling Method Study," *Stress and Health* 40, no. 5 (2024): e3424, https://online library.wiley.com/doi/10.1002/smi.3424.

108 *students who regularly got into flow during lockdowns:* Wei Liu, Wen Zhang, Dimitri van der Linden, and Arnold B. Bakker, "Flow and Flourishing During the Pandemic: The Roles of Strengths Use and Playful Design," *Journal of Happiness Studies* 24, no. 7 (2023): 2153–75, https://doi.org /10.1007/s10902-023-00670-2.

109 *so far as to suggest that fatigue goes away:* Guy Raz, "What Makes a Life Worth Living?," *TED Radio Hour*, NPR, April 17, 2015, transcript, https:// www.npr.org/transcripts/399806632.

109 *flow demands intense cognitive effort:* Morgane Pujol, Loïc Caroux, and Céline Lemercier, "Flow State Requires Effortful Attentional Control but Is Experienced Effortlessly by Video Game Players," *Interacting with Computers* 36, no. 6 (2024): 371–82, https://doi.org/10.1093/iwc/iwae026.

109 *"I had learned already never to empty the well":* Larry W. Phillips, ed., *Ernest Hemingway on Writing* (Scribner, 2002).

109 *flow stints feed life satisfaction:* Lung Hung Chen, Yun-Ci Ye, Mei-Yen chen, and I-Wu Tung, "Alegría! Flow in Leisure and Life Satisfaction: The Mediating Role of Event Satisfaction Using Data from an Acrobatics Show," *Social Indicators Research* 99, no. 2 (2010): 301–13, https://doi.org/10.1007/s11205-010-9581-z.

Chapter 8: Brief Candles

111 *When Kurt Stange was a full-time family doctor:* Kurt Stange, interviews with author, October 2024–May 2025.

113 *decades-long studies have found:* "The Good Life: A Discussion with Dr. Robert Waldinger," Harvard T.H. Chan School of Public Health, November 22, 2024, https://hsph.harvard.edu/health-happiness/news/the-good-life-a-discussion-with-dr-robert-waldinger/.

113 *described life itself as a brief candle:* William Shakespeare, *Macbeth* (Norton Critical Editions, 2016).

113 *what psychologist Carl Rogers calls "active listening":* Carl R. Rogers and Richard Evans Farson, *Active Listening* (Martino Fine Books, 2015).

114 *In a study of preschool-aged children:* A. C. Dettling, S. W. Parker, S. Lane, A. Sebanc, and M. C. Gumnar, "Quality of Care and Temperament Determine Changes in Cortisol Concentrations over the Day for Young Children in Childcare," *Psychoneuroendocrinology* 25, no. 8 (2000): 819–36, https://doi.org/10.1016/s0306-4530(00)00028-7.

114 *"thirty-second bursts of attention":* Sue C. Bratton and Garry L. Landreth, *Child-Parent Relationship Therapy Treatment Manual* (Routledge, 2020), 12–13.

114 *high levels of activity in the ventral striatum:* Hiroaki Kawamichi et al., "Perceiving Active Listening Activates the Reward System and Improves the Impression of Relevant Experiences," *Social Neuroscience* 10, no. 1 (2014): 16–26, https://doi.org/10.1080/17470919.2014.954732.

115 *Miss Kunzog, took an interest in him:* "Kurt Stange: The Thoughtful Family Doctor," *Medics Voices*, May 19, 2024, https://medicsvoices.com/kurt-stange-the-thoughtful-family-doctor/.

116 *amid record levels of medical burnout:* Dharam Kaushik, "Medical Burnout: Breaking Bad," AAMC News, June 4, 2021, https://www.aamc.org/news/medical-burnout-breaking-bad.

116 *cultivated what they called "generativity":* Johanna C. Malone, S. R. Liu, G. E. Vaillant, D. M. Rentz, and R. J. Waldinger, "Midlife Eriksonian Psychosocial Development: Setting the Stage for Late-Life Cognitive and Emotional Health," *Developmental Psychology* 52, no. 3 (2015): 496–508, https://doi.org/10.1037/a0039875.

117 *"are we looking for the candles?":* Rick Hanson, interview with author, October 2024.

117 *when you've considered the particulars of how you might do so:* Kathy Blau, Zeno Franco, and Philip G. Zimbardo, "Fostering the Heroic Imagination: An Ancient Ideal and a Modern Vision," *Eye on Psi Chi* 13, no. 3 (2009), https://doi.org/10.24839/1092-0803.Eye13.3.18.

117 *brief candle DeMarsh lit:* Tom Hallman Jr., "A Principal's 'Gift of Grace' Changed a Student's Life; 60 Years Later, a Belated Thank You in Pendleton Changed More Lives," OregonLive, December 17, 2023, https://www.oregonlive.com/pacific-northwest-news/2023/12/a-principals-gift-of-grace-changed-a-students-life-60-years-later-a-belated-thank-you-in-pendleton-changed-more-lives.html.

118 *Ting would later say of DeMarsh:* "Second Chances and Lasting Legacies," ASIJ Stories, American School in Japan, accessed July 18, 2025, https://www.asij.ac.jp/asij-stories/second-chances-and-lasting-legacies.

118 *grow more willing to help those in need:* Itziar Alonso-Arbiol, Magdalena Bobowik, Aitziber Pascual, Susana Conejero, and Sonia Padoan, "Moral Exemplars Promote Positive Attitudes, Beliefs, Intentions, and Behaviors Toward Outgroups During the COVID-19 Pandemic: The Explanatory Role of Self-Transcendent Emotions," *Group Processes & Intergroup Relations* 27, no. 1 (2023): 118–41, https://doi.org/10.1177/13684302231165730.

119 *prompt the release of . . . norepinephrine:* Rick Hanson, Shauna Shapiro, Emma Hutton-Thamm, Michael R. Hagerty, and Kevin P. Sullivan, "Learning to Learn from Positive Experiences," *Journal of Positive Psychology* 18, no. 1 (2021): 142–53, https://doi.org/10.1080/17439760.2021.2006759.

119 *Luma Mufleh made a wrong turn:* Luma Mufleh, interview with author, November 2024.

120 *a nonprofit called Fugees Family:* "Who We Are," Fugees Family (website), accessed July 2025, https://fugeesfamily.org/who-we-are/.

120 *serves more than one hundred refugee students:* "Georgia Fugees Academy Charter School," Great! Schools (website), accessed July 18, 2025, https://

www.greatschools.org/georgia/atlanta/9159-Georgia-Fugees-Academy
-Charter-School/.

Chapter 9: Selfless Pacing

123   *Ever since:* Portions of this chapter first appeared in Elizabeth Svoboda, "Why We Need to Set Boundaries on Our Generosity," *Greater Good Magazine,* November 16, 2021, https://greatergood.berkeley.edu/article/item/why_we_need_to_set_boundaries_on_our_generosity.

123   *Abby Reyes hiked Utah's majestic Escalante River Canyon:* Abby Reyes, interview with author, January 2025.

124   *rabbi Danya Ruttenberg writes:* Rabbi Danya Ruttenberg, "Who's already doing useful work in your area and what do they need? What time/talents/resources do you have to offer? What's your sphere of influence?," theradr.bsky.social post on Bluesky, December 4, 2024, 11:39 p.m., https://bsky.app/profile/theradr.bsky.social/post/3lcj4i3jkg32u.

124   *engages the brain's mesolimbic reward system:* Lynn E. O'Connor, Jack W. Berry, Thomas B. Lewis, and David J. Stiver, "Empathy-Based Pathogenic Guilt, Pathological Altruism, and Psychopathology," in *Pathological Altruism,* ed. Barbara Oakley, Ariel Knafo, Guruprasad Madhavan, and David Sloan Wilson (Oxford University Press, 2011), 19.

124   *has documented the euphoric "helper's high":* James Baraz and Shoshana Alexander, "The Helper's High," *Greater Good Magazine,* February 1, 2010, https://greatergood.berkeley.edu/article/item/the_helpers_high.

124   *Research also shows that dedicated givers are healthier:* Sara Konrath, Andrea Fuhrel-Forbis, Alina Lou, and Stephanie Brown, "Motives for Volunteering Are Associated with Mortality Risk in Older Adults," *Health Psychology* 31, no. 1 (2012): 87–96, https://pubmed.ncbi.nlm.nih.gov/21842999/.

124   *healthier blood pressure and blood glucose levels:* Jeffrey A. Burr, Sae Hwang Han, and Jane L. Tavares, "Volunteering and Cardiovascular Disease Risk: Does Helping Others Get 'Under the Skin?,'" *Gerontologist* 56, no. 5 (2015): 937–47, https://doi.org/10.1093/geront/gnv032.

124   *less likely to die over a four-year period:* Eric S. Kim, Ashley V. Whillans, Matthew T. Lee, Ying Chen, and Tyler J. VanderWeele, "Volunteering and Subsequent Health and Well-Being in Older Adults: An Outcome-Wide Longitudinal Approach," *American Journal of Preventive Medicine* 59, no. 2 (2020): 176–86, https://doi.org/10.1016/j.amepre.2020.03.004.

125 *Activism offers similar benefits:* Jerusha Osberg Conner, Emily Greytak, Carly D. Evich, and Lauren Wray-Lake, "Burnout and Belonging: How the Costs and Benefits of Youth Activism Affect Youth Health and Wellbeing," *Youth* 3, no. 1 (2023): 127–45, https://doi.org/10.3390/youth3010009.

125 *"an innate desire to make other people happy":* Barbara Oakley, interview with author, October 2021. See also Oakley et al., eds., *Pathological Altruism.*

125 *posted in a support forum:* Jennifern_, "I hate to admit it but I'm tired of revolving my life around caregiving," post on Reddit, n.d., https://www.reddit.com/r/CaregiverSupport/comments/mj3658/i_hate_to_admit_it_but_im_tired_of_revolving_my/.

126 *par for the course to put in overtime:* Jonathan Timm, "The Plight of the Overworked Nonprofit Employee," *The Atlantic*, August 24, 2016, https://www.theatlantic.com/business/archive/2016/08/the-plight-of-the-overworked-nonprofit-employee/497081/.

126 *say they rarely or never feel relaxed:* Alessandra Raimondi, "The Cost of Caregiving: Family Caregivers' Mental Health," AARP, August 29, 2023, https://www.aarp.org/pri/topics/ltss/family-caregiving/caregivers-mental-health/.

126 *the same dogged qualities that fuel engagement:* Paul Gorski, interview with author, January 2025.

127 *familiar physical signs of unaddressed pacing problems:* Cher Weixia Chen and Paul C. Gorski, "Burnout in Social Justice and Human Rights Activists: Symptoms, Causes and Implications," *Journal of Human Rights Practice* 7, no. 3 (2015): 366–90, https://doi.org/10.1093/jhuman/huv011.

128 *people made an earnest effort to serve the greater good:* Katarzyna Byrka, Katarzyna Cantarero, Dariusz Dolinski, and Wijnard Van Tilburg, "Consequences of Sisyphean Efforts: Meaningless Effort Decreases Motivation to Engage in Subsequent Conservation Behaviors through Disappointment," *Sustainability* 13, no. 10 (2021): 5716, https://doi.org/10.3390/su13105716.

128 *Maslach and her colleague Mary Gomes write:* Rachel MacNair, ed., *Working for Peace: A Handbook of Practical Psychology and Other Tools* (Impact Publishers, 2006), 43.

128 *"It's detrimental to the change we hope to achieve":* Cher Weixia Chen, interview with author, January 2025.

129 *you lose the psychological benefits:* Conner et al., "Burnout and Belonging."

129 *"we find in our subjects a healthy selfishness":* Abraham H. Maslow, *Motivation and Personality* (Harper & Row, 1954), 257.

129 *people who score highly on a "pathological altruism" scale:* Scott Barry Kaufman and Emanuel Jauk, "Healthy Selfishness and Pathological Altruism: Measuring Two Paradoxical Forms of Selfishness," *Frontiers in Psychology* 11 (May 21, 2020), https://doi.org/10.3389/fpsyg.2020 .01006.

129 *happy people are* more *likely to take action:* Kostadin Kushlev, Danielle M. Drummond, Samantha J. Heintzalman, and Ed Diener, "Do Happy People Care about Society's Problems?," *Journal of Positive Psychology* 15, no. 4 (2019): 467–77, https://doi.org/10.1080/17439760.2019.1639797.

131 *we often make decisions about service:* Barbara A. Oakley, "Concepts and Implications of Altruism Bias and Pathological Altruism," *Proceedings of the National Academy of Sciences* 110, Suppl. 2 (2013): 10408–15, https://doi .org/10.1073/pnas.1302547110.

131 *what psychologist Daniel Kahneman called "fast thinking":* Daniel Kahneman, *Thinking, Fast and Slow* (Farrar, Straus and Giroux, 2011).

132 *engages the whole group in what she calls "strategic questioning":* Fran Peavey, "Strategic Questioning: An Approach to Creating Personal and Social Change," *In Context* 40 (Spring 1995): 36, https://www.context.org/iclib /ic40/peavey/.

134 *"We need to conserve our energy so we can stay in the race":* Dylan Keese-Forster, "The Pace of Activism in an Online World," post on How to Be a Woman on the Internet, Substack, June 13, 2023, https://howtobeawoman ontheinternet.substack.com/p/the-pace-of-activism-in-an-online.

Chapter 10: Dropping off the Map

137 *It's the last:* Portions of this chapter were reported from Paris, Valensole, and Marseille, France, in July and August 2023.

138 *sociologist Jean Viard of Paris's:* Sam Schechner and Lee Harris, "What Happens When All of France Takes Vacation? 438 Miles of Traffic," *Wall Street Journal,* July 31, 2019, https://www.wsj.com/articles/what-happens-when -all-of-france-takes-vacation-438-miles-of-traffic-11564600399.

138 *University of Washington management researcher Kira Schabram:* Kira Schabram, interview with author, August 2023.

138   *diarist Etty Hillesum wrote:* Etty Hillesum, *An Interrupted Life: The Diaries, 1941–1943*; and *Letters from Westerbork*, trans. Arnold J. Pomerans (Henry Holt, 1996).

139   *fewer than 20 percent of US companies:* Joanne Sammer, "Sabbaticals Could Be the Solution to Employee Burnout," SHRM, December 21, 2023, https://www.shrm.org/topics-tools/news/benefits-compensation/sab baticals-solution-to-employee-burnout.

139   *well over half their waking hours:* Sophie Gherardi, "It's Not Fair!," Philonomist, July 2, 2025, https://www.philonomist.com/en/article/its-not -fair?embed=1.

139   *"bread, peace and liberty":* French Communist Party, "For the Respect of the Will of the People," *L'Humanité*, May 27, 1936, trans. Mitch Abidor, Marxists Internet Archive, accessed July 18, 2025, https://www.marx ists.org/history/international/comintern/sections/france/1936/respect .htm.

139   *thirty days of paid annual vacation:* "Employee Paid Leave in the Private Sector," Service-Public.fr, April 18, 2025, https://www.service-public.fr /particuliers/vosdroits/F2258?lang=en.

139   *goes well beyond the letter of the law:* Michael Mendolia, interview with author, July 2023.

140   *"Right to Disconnect":* République française, "Loi n° 2016-1088 du 8 août 2016 relative au travail, à la modernisation du dialogue social et à la sécurisation des parcours professionnels," *Journal Officiel de la République Française* 0184 (August 9, 2016), https://www.legifrance.gouv.fr/loda/id /JORFTEXT000032983213.

141   *after six years of intensive harvests:* Bai Kang and Michael T. Miller, *An Overview of the Sabbatical Leave in Higher Education: A Synopsis of the Literature Base* (1999), ERIC Document ED 430 524, https://files.eric.ed.gov/full text/ED430471.pdf.

141   *the concept became ingrained in academia:* Ibid.

141   *"During my thirteen years as president":* Walter Crosby Eells and Ernest Victor Hollis, *Sabbatical Leave in American Higher Education: Origin, Early History, and Current Practices* (US Department of Health, Education, and Welfare, Office of Education, 1962), 46.

142   *129 faculty members on sabbatical:* Oranit B. Davidson et al., "Sabbatical Leave: Who Gains and How Much?" *Journal of Applied Psychology* 95, no. 5 (2010): 953–64, https://doi.org/10.1037/a0020068.

142   *studied vacationers who took breaks:* Jessica de Bloom, Sabine A. E. Geurts, and Michiel A. J. Kompier, "Vacation (After-) Effects on Employee Health and Well-Being, and the Role of Vacation Activities, Experiences and Sleep," *Journal of Happiness Studies* 14, no. 2 (2012): 613–33, https://doi.org/10.1007/s10902-012-9345-3.

142   *Break-takers' sense of control:* Davidson et al., "Sabbatical Leave."

142   *gives its employees six full weeks off:* G. Page Singletary, "History of Sabbaticals (from The Gift of a Sabbatical Series)," post on LinkedIn, January 3, 2019, https://www.linkedin.com/pulse/gift-sabbatical-part-two-history-sabbaticals-g-page-singletary/.

143   *Benzi Schreiber embarked on his extended break:* Benzi Schreiber, "It's Just a Job: Thoughts on Leaving Intel," post on LinkedIn, September 1, 2017, https://www.linkedin.com/pulse/its-just-job-thoughts-leaving-intel-benzi-schreiber/.

143   *"I was looking for something of a nest":* Carole Schaal, interview with author, August 2023.

145   *that theme resurfaces later on:* Laure Gaillard, interview with author, August 2023.

146   *conducted in-depth interviews:* Kira Schabram, Matt Bloom, and DJ DiDonna, "Recover, Explore, Practice: The Transformative Potential of Sabbaticals," *Academy of Management Discoveries* 9, no. 4 (2022): 441–68, https://doi.org/10.5465/amd.2021.0100.

147   *promotes more recovery than a weeklong one:* de Bloom et al., "Vacation (After-) Effects."

147   *After Gonzales started a one-year break:* Alysia Gonzales, interview with author, January 2025.

149   *Gray toiled at her job in the healthcare sector:* Vanessa Gray, interview with author, October 2024.

Chapter 11: Collective Pacing

153   *"Today we're going to talk about developing and assessing trust":* Portions of this chapter were reported on-site from Brown University, Providence, Rhode Island, November 2023.

154   *"the best boundaries in the world":* Leah Weiss, interview with author, November 2022.

154   *members also report better psychological health:* Linda J. Roberts et al.,
       "Giving and Receiving Help: Interpersonal Transactions in Mutual-Help
       Meetings and Psychosocial Adjustment of Members," *American Journal of
       Community Psychology* 27, no. 6 (1999): 841–68, https://doi.org/10.1023
       /a:1022214710054.

154   *the less burnout those members suffer:* Wenxin Wang et al., "Teamwork
       Quality and Health Workers Burnout Nexus: A New Insight from Canon-
       ical Correlation Analysis," *Human Resources for Health* 20, no. 1 (2022),
       https://doi.org/10.1186/s12960-022-00734-z.

155   *"I'm going to throw up":* Elizabeth Svoboda, "Moral Injury Is an Invisible
       Epidemic That Affects Millions," *Scientific American,* September 19, 2022,
       https://www.scientificamerican.com/article/moral-injury-is-an-invisible
       -epidemic-that-affects-millions/.

156   *"toxic workplace" traits like rudeness:* Amna Anjum, Xu Ming, Ahmed
       Faisal Siddiqi, and Samma Faiz Rasool, "An Empirical Study Analyzing
       Job Productivity in Toxic Workplace Environments," *International Journal
       of Environmental Research and Public Health* 15, no. 5 (2018): 1035, https://
       doi.org/10.3390/ijerph15051035.

156   *don't understand how to foster collective flourishing:* Daryl Appleton, inter-
       view with author, May 2023.

156   *wellness interventions did not measurably boost:* Zirui Song and Katherine
       Baicker, "Effect of a Workplace Wellness Program on Employee Health
       and Economic Outcomes," *JAMA* 321, no. 15 (2019): 1491, https://doi.org
       /10.1001/jama.2019.3307.

158   *urges trainees to approach him and Appleton:* Ken Lynch, interview with au-
       thor, May 2023.

160   *about three-quarters of respondents:* Jennifer Robison, "Turning Around
       Employee Turnover," *Gallup Business Journal,* May 8, 2008, https://news
       .gallup.com/businessjournal/106912/turning-around-your-turnover
       -problem.aspx.

161   *supportive social groups often thrive better:* Arne Traulsen and Martin A.
       Nowak, "Evolution of Cooperation by Multilevel Selection." *PNAS* 103,
       no. 29 (2006): 10952–55, https://doi.org/10.1073/pnas.0602530103.

162   *initial data show burnout rates dropping:* Chelsey Ciambella et al., "Burnt
       Out, Now What? General Surgery Residents Experience with Burnout and
       Implementation of Department Sponsored Wellness Program," Program

Abstracts, New England Surgical Society Annual Meeting, 2022, https:// meeting.nesurgical.org/program/2022/22.cgi.

163 *consultants ran with a forty-person team:* Tony Schwartz, Rene Pelizzi, Kelly Gruber, and Emily Pines, "What Happens When Teams Fight Burnout Together," *Harvard Business Review,* September 30, 2019, https://hbr.org /2019/09/what-happens-when-teams-fight-burnout-together.

164 *One way to foster such supportive environments:* Sarah Milby, interview with author, February 2023.

164 *"spill over" and create broader cultural changes:* Lina Koppel et al., "Individual-Level Solutions May Support System-Level Change—If They Are Internalized as Part of One's Social Identity," *Behavioral and Brain Sciences* 46 (January 1, 2023), https://doi.org/10.1017/s0140525x2300105x.

Chapter 12: The New Pacing Movement

167 *stages a reimagined kind of service:* The Nap Ministry, "A Moment at the Rest Temple," post on Instagram, April 19, 2023, https://www.instagram .com/p/CrO08lNxvLE/.

167 *hosted a rest-themed book group:* "Rest Is Resistance Book Group with Tricia Hersey," poster as appeared on StayHappening, NYU Center for Black Virtual Culture at IAAA, November 16, 2023, https://stayhappening.com /e/rest-is-resistance-book-group-with-tricia-hersey-E3LV2QYOJCV2.

167 *an outdoor "collective daydreaming" event:* "Collective Daydreaming Activation with the Nap Ministry," Wa Na Wari Seattle, YouTube video, 1:56:23, August 13, 2022, https://www.youtube.com/watch?v=dycU2UA1RhY.

168 *Hersey said at a recent event:* "Rest Is Resistance—Featuring: Tricia Hersey," California Faculty Association, YouTube video, 1:26:19, January 15, 2025, https://www.youtube.com/watch?v=vmtRo2SDoVg.

168 *"times that demand complex thoughts and conversations":* Jenny Odell, *How to Do Nothing: Resisting the Attention Economy* (Melville House, 2019), x.

168 *"It could be a marathon, it could be a sprint":* Carl Honoré, interview with author, March 2024.

168 *"it is nothing but work, work, work":* Tom Flinders, *Henry David Thoreau: Spiritual and Prophetic Writings* (Orbis Books, 2015).

169 *the Slow Food movement:* Carlo Petrini, *Slow Food: The Case for Taste* (Columbia University Press, 2003).

170 *his first book* In Praise of Slowness: Carl Honoré, *In Praise of Slowness: Challenging the Cult of Speed* (HarperOne, 2004).

170 *His viral TED Talk on the topic:* Carl Honoré, "In Praise of Slowness," TED Talk, July 2005, https://www.ted.com/talks/carl_honore_in_praise_of _slowness.

170 *she felt continually overworked:* Melonyce McAfee, "The Nap Bishop Is Spreading the Good Word: Rest," *New York Times*, October 13, 2022, https://www.nytimes.com/2022/10/13/well/live/nap-ministry-bishop -tricia-hersey.html.

170 *planned a performance art piece called* Transfiguration: Tricia Hersey, interview by Ayana Young, "Tricia Hersey on Rest as Resistance [Encore]," *For The Wild*, episode 267, originally aired June 2020, rebroadcast July 20, 2025, podcast transcript, https://forthewild.world/podcast-transcripts /tricia-hersey-on-rest-as-resistance-encore-267.

171 *Atlanta art installation called* A Resting Place: "About the Nap Ministry," Nap Ministry, 2021, https://thenapministry.wordpress.com/about/.

171 *her newest book,* We Will Rest! The Art of Escape: Tricia Hersey, *We Will Rest! The Art of Escape,* illus. George McCalman (Little, Brown Spark, 2024).

171 *going through her own rest-related epiphany:* Jo Hawkes, interview with author, April 2023.

173 *worker Crystal Guo told a reporter:* Goh Chiew Tong, "'I Accept Being Ordinary': China's Youth Are Turning Their Backs on Hustle Culture," *CNBC Make It*, October 10, 2022, https://www.cnbc.com/2022/09/16 /china-youth-reject-hustle-culture-face-unemployment-economic-uncer tainty.html.

173 *fellow junior employees threatened to strike:* Sunny Nagpaul, "A 35-Year-Old Junior Bank of America Associate Suddenly Died—and It's Ignited Discussions About Wall Street's Intense Working Conditions," *Fortune*, May 8, 2024, https://fortune.com/2024/05/08/leo-lukenas-iii-bank-of-america -junior-investment-banker-death-wall-street-working-conditions/.

174 *gone up fourfold within just a year:* Roya Zeitoune and Nicolas Szmidt, "'Slow Living': The New Consumer Trend," Think with Google, April 17, 2025, https://business.google.com/us/think/consumer-insights/covid-slow -living-trend/.

174 *Bill Gates said in a 2023 commencement address:* Sydney Lake, "Bill Gates 'Didn't Believe in Vacations' and Worked on the Weekends While Building

Microsoft—but Regretted It. Here Are His 3 Tips for Success," Yahoo! Finance, December 18, 2024, https://finance.yahoo.com/news/bill-gates -didn-t-believe-020600945.html.

176   *her grandmother, who worked two jobs:* Tricia Hersey, interview by Ayana Young, *For The Wild*, episode 185, originally aired June 2020, podcast audio transcript, https://forthewild.world/podcast-transcripts/tricia-hersey-on -rest-as-resistance-185.

176   *complete them—but to do so by fulfilling:* modernmommydoc, post on Instagram, video, October 17, 2024. https://www.instagram.com/reel/DBNE HjMyGVG/.

Conclusion: Course Corrections

181   *set her sights on climbing the marketing world's ranks:* Michele Benoit, interviews with author, March 2021–December 2024. One of Benoit's quotes also appears in Elizabeth Svoboda, "The Evolutionary Reason All Your Friends Made Babies During the Pandemic," *Inverse*, April 1, 2021, https://www.inverse.com/mind-body/pandemic-life-changes-sci ence-psychology.

184   *"not the discharge of tension at any cost":* Viktor Frankl, *Man's Search for Meaning*, trans. Ilse Lasch (Beacon Press, 2006).

187   *"authentic and well within your human limits":* Rosie Spinks, "Wild Early Drafts," What Do We Do Now That We're Here, Substack, December 13, 2024, https://rojospinks.substack.com/p/wild-early-drafts.

187   *calling out lapses in integrity:* Steven J. Huddart and Hong Qu, *Rotten Apples and Sterling Examples: Moral Reasoning and Peer Influences on Honesty in Managerial Reporting*, AAA 2013 Management Accounting Section (MAS) Meeting Paper, last revised November 13, 2023, https://ssrn.com /abstract=2133072.

About the Author

Elizabeth Svoboda is an award-winning journalist and contributing writer for the *Boston Globe*'s Ideas section. Her work has appeared in *Scientific American, Discover, Atlas Obscura, Greater Good Magazine,* and *The New York Times,* as well as in *The Best American Science and Nature Writing* anthology. She is the author of *What Makes a Hero? The Surprising Science of Selflessness* (Current, 2013) and *The Life Heroic: How to Unleash Your Most Amazing Self* (Zest Books, 2019). Her reporting has taken her from marathon starting lines to redwood canopies and compassion-training classes. She lives in San Jose, California, with her husband and two young sons.